WALLS, FLOORS and CEILINGS

WALLS, FLOORS

How to Repair, Renovate and Decorate the Interior Surfaces of Your Home

A Popular Science Book

and CEILINGS

Jackson Hand

Drawings by
Carl J. De Groote

POPULAR SCIENCE

HARPER & ROW

New York, Evanston, San Francisco, London

Times Mirror Magazines, Inc.
Book Division
Editor and Publisher John W. Sill
Executive Editor Henry Gross
Associate Editor Neil Soderstrom
Art Director Jeff Fitschen
Production Manager Millicent La Roque
Editorial Assistants Pat Blair
Ellen Patrisso

Library of Congress Catalog Card Number: 74:33574
ISBN: 0-06-011772-9

Manufactured in the United States of America

Contents

Introduction

The walls, floors, and ceilings of our homes form the background for our domestic lives. The way they are finished and decorated reflects our personality and our reaction to constantly changing ideas in home decor. And, in so doing, they contribute to our environment for living.

It is because of the visual (as well as vitally functional) aspects of walls, floors, and ceilings that a tremendous number of new products have come along in recent years, aimed at making them more interesting, more functional, and easier for the do-it-yourselfer to install. Among these new products and methods are:

● Prefinished paneling that never needs any maintenance other than normal cleaning.

● Self-stick wall materials enabling you to reproduce the exact look of brick, stone, and other masonry materials—some of them actually made of thin sheets or pieces of masonry, unitized so they can be put up in small sheets.

● Tiling materials for bathroom and kitchen that do the job better than older materials requiring the skills and equipment of professional tiling crews.

● Methods of providing wall-to-wall ceiling illumination for the best room lighting possible. Acoustical ceilings, too.

● Maintenance-free flooring materials with the look of tile, marble, wood, brick—you name it—that anybody can put down in a typical room on a typical Saturday. In addition, true wood flooring is taking on new forms. There are parquet units as easy to lay as floor tile. For a quick-and-easy new wood look, you'll find thin strip flooring that goes down with adhesive (over the weekend) on top of any existing wood floor that is sound.

● Paints and enamels and clear finishes that continually become easier to use and more durable—for walls, trim, ceilings, floors.

Best of all, while the materials you need for walls, floors, and ceilings get easier to use and better in performance, their cost stays low on a do-it-yourself basis. For example, you can completely change the mood of a room for the price of a couple of gallons of wall paint or a few rolls of wallpaper. On the other hand, you can do over a room with matched architectural-grade paneling at $100 or more a sheet.

All of these materials and many more will be covered on the following pages, along with information vital to the householder who wants to do the work himself either for pure personal satisfaction, or because he can't find anyone else to do it at any price.

Included are discussions of the following basics:

● The way walls are built—you'll need to know if you have any serious repairs to do or if you want to put in a new partition.

● How stairs are made—necessary knowledge for silencing a squeaky tread or two.

● The basics of floor joists, stretchers, subflooring, and underlayment—all of importance when you want to put down a new surface or jack up a sagging floor.

Throughout the book you'll find extensive use of photographs and drawings to help explain the technicalities and the techniques of repair, maintenance, and new construction. And, every effort has been made to cover *everything you need to know to do a job within the scope of a home handyman*. On the other hand, if it is a job that takes more skills or tools than most of us have, you won't find it here. When that's the case, call in a specialist from the yellow pages.

The tools recommended are those you'll find in the toolbox of most fix-it-minded homeowners. For some jobs, however, specialized tools may be essential. If you don't have such a tool, can't find a substitute for it, and don't wish to make a purchase, you'll find the solution to your problem at a tool rental outfit; they are unbelievably well stocked. Plan your work carefully so as to make most efficient use of the tool, and you'll be pleased at the increased versatility you can rent for a few dollars.

Part 1

The Development of
Wall-Surfacing Materials

When our forefathers built their first homes on colonial soil, the inside wall was literally the inner surface of the outside wall. If the house happened to be logs, what you got were logs and the chinking between them. If it happened to be a stone house, the inside wall was the back side of the stones. Quite often, a house was built with a view to good looks inside and the outside was left to chance.

One of the first home improvements was the addition of a plaster surfacing on the inside of the walls, both to make them look better and to improve their weatherproofness. The results were rough and uneven. It was not until lumber—sawn boards —became the standard building material that interior walls began to achieve the smoothness and attractiveness that evolved into today's slick surfaces.

If the house you live in is quite old, chances are that the walls are constructed in a form of the stud wall discussed in the following chapter. The oldest plaster walls were lath and plaster. This is the surface technique that involves narrow strips of rough-sawn wood called "lath" nailed to

the studs with a little space between the strips. Old-time plasterers troweled on a rough coat of plaster, which oozed between the lath strips and was itself held in place not only by the adhesion of the mortar, but also by the beads between the lath. Then, they troweled on a finish coat of lighter, smoother mix for the final surface.

If your house is somewhat newer, the carpenters who built it may have bypassed wood lath in favor of metal lath or a sheet-plaster lath substitute. The sheets—usually 16 inches by 2 feet—were nailed to the studs, forming the basis for finish plaster.

More recently, the construction method called "drywall" has pretty well taken over the field. This system uses big (4x8 feet or longer) sheets of gypsum board, smooth and ready for paint or paper on the face side. The sheets go up with special nails. The joints disappear under smooth application of a spackle material. The drywall system is not only fast and economical in original construction, but it is easiest for the average householder to repair or replace.

Although most drywall surfacing is the basis for paint or paper, some gypsum

The biggest advantage of gypsum board as a wall surface is speed and ease of handling. Big sheets go up with nails or adhesives or both, and no special framing is required beyond stud spacing that hits 48-inch modules.

board materials are faced with vinyl sheets in various colors, patterns, and textures which will give you an attractive finished wall that will last practically forever—easy to keep clean, never requiring refinishing.

PANELED WALLS

Another wall-surfacing method we inherit from the colonial interior decorators is paneling. It was used extensively, even earlier than plastering, because the materials

and the installation techniques were easier to come by. The same is true today, making paneling very popular as a do-it-yourself wall.

In the oldest construction, paneling was most often in the form of standard thickness boards. The edges were usually half-lap or tongue-and-groove. This not only kept the boards lined up, but also accommodated any shrink-and-swell which would, without the tongue, result in wide gaps between boards during the dry season. The oldest form of board paneling had beveled edges which formed a V-groove where the boards joined and helped conceal the joint. Later, the boards had the beveled edges, but one edge also had a shaped molding. This obscured the joint even more thoroughly and added a bit of decoration. It is still used today; it is called "novelty" paneling.

Now and then, an old house may have been dignified with "raised paneling," an elegant and lovely combination of vertical stiles and horizontal crossmembers and wide, selected boards with flat beveled edges. The wood used for paneling was, normally, a local, convenient wood—most often pine—usually painted.

Our forefathers most often nailed their paneling at the top and bottom of the wall, covering the nail heads with a molding. Board-thickness paneling in later years was nailed to furring strips, just as is done today. Furring strips are 1x2s nailed horizontally to the studs, generally spaced about 16 inches apart, with one at the ceiling, one at the floor.

It is not uncommon to find such paneling in the form of a wainscot, the name given to paneling that covers only the lower part of the wall. The result served the dual purpose of good looks and extra protection for that part of the wall most exposed to dirt and

Sheet materials can have all the appearance of individual boards, as is the case with this synthetic, prefinished material from Georgia-Pacific.

Textured plywood paneling has the look of old barnboard, and is available in several different colors. Courtesy U. S. Plywood

The look of raised paneling is possible in modern decorating, as illustrated by this pattern in a room filled with glass furniture and modernized 18th century French chairs. Courtesy Masonite Corp.

wear and tear. In contemporary wall treatments, the wainscot principle is still widely used, for both functional and decorative purposes.

Sheet-form paneling. Most paneling put up in recent years is in sheet form — sometimes full 4x8 feet or longer, sometimes in narrower strips, to match standard stud spacing. Usually the edges are tongue-and-groove, and the pattern of the material is such that the joint disappears in a V-groove or other feature.

The materials used for sheet paneling include plywood, hardboard, some plastics, and certain molded novelty patterns. The sheet thickness is most often $1/4$-inch. The face may be prefinished. Some patterns are extremely true imitations of barnboard, wormy chestnut, and other rare materials.

In addition to these more common household wall-facing items, there are murals, various forms of self-stick bricks and tiles, genuine tiles, and even materials not intended for wall use — but often very decorative and useful. All of these are covered — their installation, maintenance, and repair — in later chapters.

2

How Walls Are Built

If you are lucky, you may never see the inside of a wall; you may never encounter repairs so extensive that removal of the wall surfacing material is necessary. However, even for home improvement projects as simple as hanging a picture, it helps to know how the typical residential wall is put together. And there may come the day when you'll want to add a partition somewhere in the house—perhaps to subdivide a bedroom, or install a closet across the end of a room, or make use of attic or basement space.

STANDARD WALL FUNCTIONS

Walls have several basic functions in addition to dividing one area from another.

1. They may provide support for the roof, for ceilings and, in multistory buildings, for upper floors.

2. They may provide insulation against heat or cold, as well as acoustical barriers between rooms or between the quiet of indoors and the racket of outside.

3. They provide a base and background for decoration, either the color of paint or the pattern of the wallpaper, or as the place to hang works of art.

4. They provide support for hanging shelves, cupboards, medicine cabinets and other features.

To perform these functions, a wall must be rigid and rugged. And it must have a surface suited to its decorative role. (This skin may also contribute heavily to rigidity and ruggedness.)

Most walls—almost *all* walls—in today's houses are constructed of wooden 2x4s. There is a growing trend toward the use of structural members made of aluminum or steel. As this move toward metals in residential construction increases, the day may come when your lumberyard carries the elements you need to put up metal framing. When this day arrives, you'll be switching over to self-tapping screws and pop rivets in addition to nails and spikes. But the elements will be the same, the structural procedures the same, the dimensions the same, though the results may perhaps be truer and more stable.

7

HOW A WALL GOES UP

Even though you may never build a wall from scratch, it will be useful to know how the job is done. In other words, it is easier to understand what is inside a wall if you know the various members involved and understand both why they were used and how they were put together.

Except in extremely rare cases, walls go up after the rough floor is laid, and the floor acts as a work platform. This is true both in original construction and in remodeling. The builder started with a floor atop the foundation. He put the walls together working on that floor. Then, if the building involved two or more floors, he put down the second-story floor and built upward from there.

If you have ever watched a house going up, you may have noticed that nine times out of ten, the walls are constructed "on the flat"—that is, lying on the floor. When the wall framing is complete, the carpenters stand it up in place. Whenever possible, you should put up a partition or a new wall in your home the same way. The only time you would go to the extra bother of constructing a wall piece by piece, in place, would be when the floor area is too small to accommodate the new wall on the flat.

The standard residential wall is composed of the following components:

Sole Plate. This is the 2x4 that runs along the floor at the bottom of the wall.

Studs. These are the vertical 2x4s that form the skeleton of the wall itself. They are almost always spaced 16 inches on center—but some walls are built with the studs 24 inches on center. In both situations there is an exact spacing of 48 inches —every other stud in the wider spacing, every third stud in the 16-inch spacing. This is to accommodate the standard 48-inch width of a wide range of structural and facing materials.

Top Plate. This is the counterpart of the sole plate, running along the top of the wall.

Fire-bars. These are short lengths of 2x4 spiked between the studs. They are sometimes called "fire stops," and their main function is to prevent updrafts through the wall from contributing to the spread of flames in case of fire. As the sketch shows, they are staggered—not in a straight line—to make end nailing easy.

If your project involves putting up a new wall, there are basic steps you must follow. These steps are covered below in what might be called standard procedure, although individual jobs may require some simple modifications.

Step one. Measure carefully between the two walls that will flank the new wall, and cut the sole plate to that length. If the distance is not too great, you'll be able to get it out of a single length of 2x4. If it is more than 16 or 18 feet, you'll need a splice. The easy way to establish the length of the long sole plate is to place two pieces of 2x4 side by side, one butted against one side wall, the other against the other. Make a mark at the end of one 2x4 and cut the excess off the other 2x4. Splice them together with a short length of 2x4 as shown in the photograph. (The job will be easiest, over all, if you position this splice so that it falls between two studs, even though this may require cutting a piece off both of the 2x4s you put on the floor to "scribe" the length.)

Make another unit the same length for the plate. This assumes, of course, that the house was constructed true and square originally, and the distance across the ceiling is the same as the distance across the floor. If it is not, you must make the sole and top plates different lengths.

Important: If the plates must be spliced,

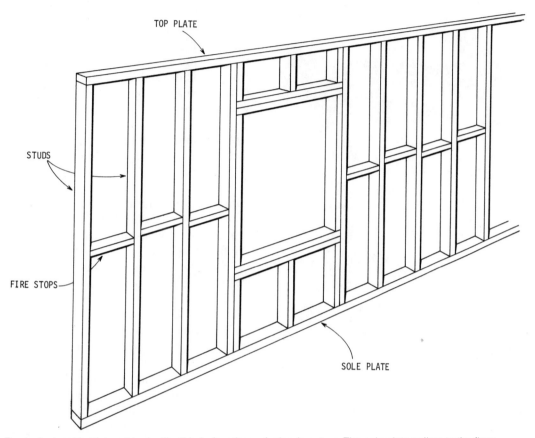

TOP PLATE

STUDS

FIRE STOPS

SOLE PLATE

The typical residential wall looks like this before the surfacing is put up. The sole plate spikes to the floor, the top plate to the ceiling, and the end studs to flanking walls.

put the splices at opposite ends so that one is not directly over the other.

Step two. Determine the length the studs must be — i.e., the distance from ceiling to floor minus twice the thickness of the 2x4 you are using for the two plates. Figuring one stud at each adjacent wall and one every 16 inches (or 24 inches, if the wall is to be with the studs 24 inches on center), cut the studs you'll need. It may be that there is more or less sag in the ceiling, and this would suggest that studs should therefore be cut in different lengths. However, unless the sag is great, you'll find that when you

stand the wall up, you'll be able to force the wall into position, and this will tend to correct the sag.

Step three. Place the plates on edge, a stud's length distance apart. At the exact ends, spike through the plates into the ends of one of the studs, using two 16-penny spikes for each joint. Measure over 16 inches and spike another stud in place. Put another at 32 inches. Position the fourth stud so that *its center is exactly 48 inches from the ends* of the plates.

Starting at the *center* of that stud, make a series of marks exactly 16 inches apart

When a wall is too long for standard 2x4 lengths, splice two together with a scrap of 2x4 at least 12 inches long, with two spikes through the cleat into the plate on each side of the joint.

Construct a wall on the floor whenever possible—then stand it in place. Use this technique for spiking through the plates into the ends of the studs.

across the length of both plates. From now on, the studs will be centered on those 16-inch marks. There will be 48 inches between a stud and the one three spaces away from it. This establishes the 48-inch progression that accommodates the 48-inch width of the majority of wall-facing materials.

At the other end, the final stud in the 16-inch progression is highly unlikely to be exactly 16 inches from the wall. If it is within 6 or 8 inches from the end, you can eliminate it entirely. But if it is one of the studs *in the 48-inch progression* it must be spiked in place to provide support for the edge of the facing material.

Of course, you must install a stud at the end of the plates.

These instructions are based on studs spaced 16 inches on center. If you are building your wall with the 24-inch spacing, the 48-inch progression will be every other stud, not every third stud.

It is not often that you'll build a wall that is nothing more than studs, one end to the other. Most of the time there will be framing for a door or a window or both. The accompanying sketches show how such openings are framed. It is important to maintain the 16-inch (or 24-inch) and the 48-inch progression over doors and windows and under windows, to provide a base for surfacing materials as they surround the opening.

The final step is to cut the fire-bars and nail them in place. By staggering them as shown in the sketch, you'll be able to end-nail into all of them except the ends of the two that fall in the spaces next to the existing walls. Toe-nail at these two points.

So—you end up with a wall lying on the floor. To stand it up, you may need to enlist the help of a friendly neighbor, although a wall that is 10 or 12 feet long can be a one-

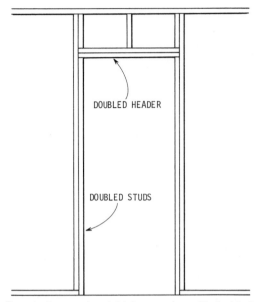

To make the opening rigid, frame a door with doubled 2x4s on either side and overhead. Dimensions for door openings are usually determined by preassembled door kits sold at lumberyards.

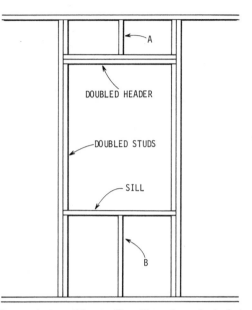

Frame windows this way. The sill can be a single 2x4 except in windows over 36 inches in width; then it should be doubled. Doubled studs flank the window. Studs *A* and *B* must be positioned to fall in with the spacing of studs in the rest of the wall.

person job. An important consideration in a partition you build in an existing dwelling is the final positioning of the wall. It is dependent on two factors.

First, of course, is the size of the two areas to be partitioned by the new wall.

Second is the location of framing members in the existing walls and the ceiling, since the new partition must be fastened to the adjoining walls, to the ceiling, and to the floor — simple enough, because it is a continuous surface.

Your biggest concern is at the ceiling. If the ceiling joists run at right angles to the new wall, positioning is no problem since you can spike up through the plate into the joists. If, however, the ceiling joists run parallel to the new wall, you can spike into an overhead joist only if the position of the wall coincides with the joist. Unless it

Prefabricated doors and windows such as this sliding unit from Anderson Windows are available at building supply outlets. They make doors and windows easy; all you do is frame wall openings to accept them.

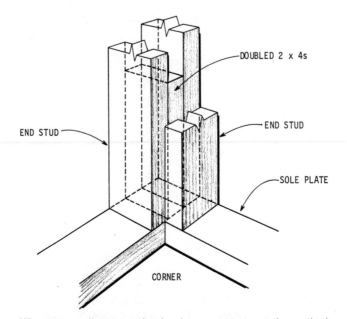

DOUBLED 2 x 4s

END STUD

END STUD

SOLE PLATE

CORNER

When your wall construction involves a corner, use the method shown here. The walls are constructed as usual, then spiked together with a doubled stud as joining element. The doubled stud does not need to run floor-to-ceiling; the joint is strong enough with its right-angled 2x4s. If you like, use three doubled 2x4s about 16 inches long, one at the floor, one at the ceiling, one in between.

would interfere greatly with the functions of the two partitioned areas, it is best to position the wall so that it is directly beneath a joist, and you can spike into it. You will find that with standard 16-inch-on-center spacing of the ceiling joists, you would have to move the wall no more than 8 inches one way or the other to locate it beneath a joist. And, in most situations, the area on one side or the other of the partition could spare that much space.

At the walls, it is best if you can spike through the end studs into studs in the existing wall. However, if working to a ceiling joist puts your wall between studs, there is an acceptable solution.

Spike at an angle into the sole and top plates of the existing wall. This will keep the new wall from skidding at the top or bottom. Then, if you feel that there might be too much flexibility in the wall between the plates, cut one more stud and spike it inside the end stud, giving it the effective stiffness of a 4x4.

You can always spike through the sole plate into the floor. Sometimes you can spike into the floor joists for additional stability.

Step four. When you have established the location of the wall, stretch a chalk line across the ceiling at the point and snap it to mark the line where the top of the wall will be.

Lift the preassembled wall up and move

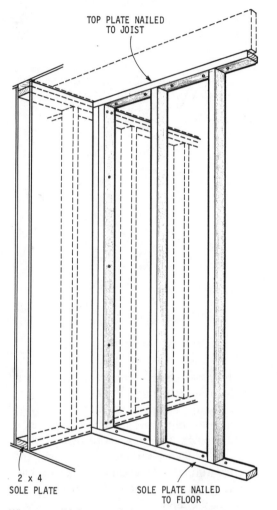

TOP PLATE NAILED TO JOIST

2 x 4 SOLE PLATE

SOLE PLATE NAILED TO FLOOR

When a wall joins an existing wall and must be positioned between studs, use the technique shown here. Spike the end stud to the plates of the adjacent wall; then spike a 2x4 inside the end stud. This gives you the effective rigidity of a 4x4.

it around until the plate is at or close to the chalk mark on the ceiling. The wall will be at a slight angle. Move the bottom in, to decrease the angle, holding the top at the chalkline above.

When things start to fit tightly use whatever force is required to make the wall vertical, and line up the plate with the chalkline above. When the wall is plumb and true, spike it into place.

Sometimes there isn't room in the area being divided to build the new wall on the floor, then stand it up. When that is the case, you must build the wall in place. Start by preparing the top and sole plates, and cut the required number of studs to length as covered above in on-the-floor construction. Then follow these steps:

● Spike the sole plate in place.

● Spike one end stud in place, resting on the sole plate at the bottom.

● Put one end of the plate on the top of that stud, which will hold it while you perform the next step.

● Measure out exactly 8 feet from the wall and put another stud in place. Toe-nail it at the bottom. Raise the plate and rest it on top of this stud. That way, it will be supported while you spike it to the ceiling.

● Install the remainder of the studs, maintaining the 16-inch (or 24-inch) on-center spacing.

With the wall framing up, you are now ready for the surfacing material.

3

Choosing a Wall Surface

With such a wide variety of wall-surfacing materials to choose from these days, the decision as to which is best becomes a bit difficult. Three factors are involved:

● Appearance is most often first. You have to live with the walls, and you might as well enjoy them.

● Function is a factor, also. In some cases the surfacing material may play a part in the rigidity of the wall. In fact, there are construction methods which take advantage of the surfacing material to provide the major part of the structural strength.

● Maintenance is important. In some areas the need for cleaning may be frequent (over a fireplace); in others difficult (over a kitchen range). The choice tightens when you consider the selection of a paint or wallpaper for its washability vs. pure beauty. And it tightens even more when it becomes necessary to consider probable physical damage to a wall—such as it might encounter in a small child's room.

THE BASIC WALL IS GYPSUM BOARD

The most popular and most used of all wall-surfacing materials these days is gypsum board—the product made by several companies, but most commonly spoken of as Sheetrock, the trade name of U.S. Gypsum. It is an easy material to work with, well within the handyman range of most homeowners, as you will discover in the following chapter.

Sheetrock is a sheet of plaster faced on both sides with paper. The face side is smooth and ready for painting or for sizing and wallpapering. The back is less smooth. The ends are raw. The edges are slightly depressed, to make it easier to make the joints invisible. The sheets are standard 4x8 feet in size, although you can get shorter or longer lengths when a ceiling runs over or under the common 8 feet in height.

In addition to the paper-smooth surface

Although gypsum board is intended basically as a smooth wall surface for painting or papering, you can buy the board surfaced with vinyl plastic in many different patterns. Patterns are reproduced by means of photo-lithography, such as the wood grain shown here in a Georgia-Pacific sheet.

for painting or wallpapering, gypsum boards also come with prefinished surfaces, plastic facing in patterns that make the sheet itself the final finish, much like paneling. Check at your building supply dealer or a paneling specialist for the various patterns and surfaces available in gypsum board.

Two thicknesses are common in gypsum board. The $1/2$-inch sheets are, of course, more rigid than the $3/8$-inch version. But, they are heavier and harder for the weekend worker to handle. The $1/2$-inch sheets, therefore, are most commonly used when the studs are spaced 24 inches apart. The $3/8$-inch material is normally heavy enough

Gypsum board walls can be given extra drama by techniques such as this. Pre-painted wooden moldings form rectangles on plain painted surfaces and surround papered areas.

for 16-inch stud spacing. In some heavy-duty applications, two layers of ³/₈-inch may be used, the second one cemented and nailed over the first.

THE MANY CHOICES IN PANELING

The selection in paneling is almost limitless, both as to materials and design. It starts with wood on one end of the scale, and runs into plastic laminates — such as Formica — on the other end. It can be raw wood or wood already treated with a finish more beautiful and durable than most of us

would want to attempt on so large a surface.

Your choice will be influenced by all the factors covered at the opening of this chapter — appearance, function, maintenance. Even more important may be the problems of installation. Some types are carpentry, pure and simple. Others require special installation techniques.

Wood paneling — that is, actual boards — is most common in tongue-and-groove pine. It is usually fairly well filled with knots for two reasons. First, it provides an outlet for the upper lengths of timber in the tree,

The standard V-groove look of knotty pine paneling is embellished here with surface-mounted pine molding finished with the same stain as the paneling. This treatment does much the same thing for solid-wood paneling as it does for gypsum board in the preceding photograph.

where the knots are. Second, it gives a pine-paneled wall an interesting look.

You can buy pine paneling with the edges shaped to form a joint-hiding V. You can buy it with molded, shaped edges. You can buy it in nominal 4-, 6-, 8-, 10-, and sometimes 12-inch widths. This permits either uniform board paneling or random widths — considered more interesting by many homeowners.

There are numerous other solid-board paneling materials, including rough-sawn cedar, redwood, barn board and a shed full

of samples of other woods and textures your lumber dealer can show you — although he may not carry the more remote items in stock.

Solid-board paneling is not ordinarily provided with a finish already on it. This means you must apply an interior enamel or a stain followed by varnish or some other transparent finish. The end product can be extremely durable, easy to clean, good for the life of the house. On the other hand, some of the rough-sawn materials are beautiful with no finish whatsoever, although

Rough-sawn ponderosa pine with a slightly darkening stain provides the good, strong look of real wood. The texture and grain pattern provide the design; you need no trim other than picture molding, baseboard, and other functional types of trim.

Materials generally thought of as intended for outdoor use are finding their way indoors. One is western red cedar bevel siding. Its natural deep-brown color is an excellent background for accessories and hangings of any color.

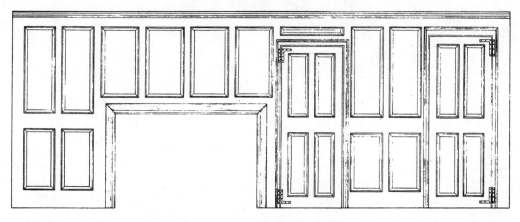
If you love the traditional and happen to live in the older-settled areas of the country, you may find genuine antique paneling advertised in local papers or in publications specializing in antiques.

they may accumulate enough dirt over a period of time so they must eventually be given a cleanable finish.

Plywood paneling. Provides a great deal more variety than solid wood. Many of the exotic species, ranging from ebony to teak to satinwood to walnut and mahogany are available at prices much lower than the solid material would cost. You can find some of the wood textured, although the graining or saw marks are not as deep or

pronounced as they are in solid wood; the plywood sheet is not thick enough to accommodate them.

V-grooving is common in plywood paneling, usually artificially produced in modules of 16 inches, to make it possible for you to fasten sheets to 16-inch-spaced studs with the nail heads buried in the grooves. Some plywood paneling has its face material carefully matched for the best effect. Other styles are made with the exact appearance of side-by-side boards.

Novel and interesting use of plywood paneling is this checkerboard of woods of similar character, yet different color. Combinations might include maple and cherry, walnut and ash, mahogany and avodire. A subtler, simpler effect would be the use of only one wood, alternating the grain direction. The squares go up with mastic.

A tremendous advantage with plywood paneling—as with hardboard, covered below—is that it comes prefinished. Of course, you can buy it raw, then put on the finish that suits your needs, and it may save you some money. The best way to do this is to finish the sheets on the flat, before they go up, thus providing yourself with the effect of "custom prefinished" material.

You buy plywood paneling either in 4x8 or longer sheets, or in 16-inch-width strips. (There are 24-inch widths in some faces, also.) You'll find several different methods of installation, covered in a later chapter.

Hardboard paneling. Made of the well-known material you see most often in a dark brown mottle, smooth on one side, with a burlaplike back. It is made by several companies, and as is true with so many products, one of the companies has pro-vided a commonly used name for the prod-uct—Masonite. Hardboard is made by a process similar to that used in making paper. Wood—often scrap unusable for other purposes—is ground into fine par-ticles and fibers, then mixed with a binder liquid. This mixture feeds into a machine which runs it between two closely spaced rollers. Out comes a "web" of material, and it undergoes additional "calendering" until it is the right thickness and density. Dura-bility, moisture resistance, and other fac-tors are controlled in the sheet by the for-mulation of the binder and by the degree of density produced by the calendering process.

Hardboard paneling is available in many different textures ranging from simulated rough sawn lumber to simulated ceramic tile. Such textures are produced by using one of the rollers as a "mold" which im-

The hardboard process makes it possible to reproduce almost any texture, even that of old, rough-sawn boards. The sheets are prefinished with a color that goes with the texturing. This is Marlite's "Weatherboard."

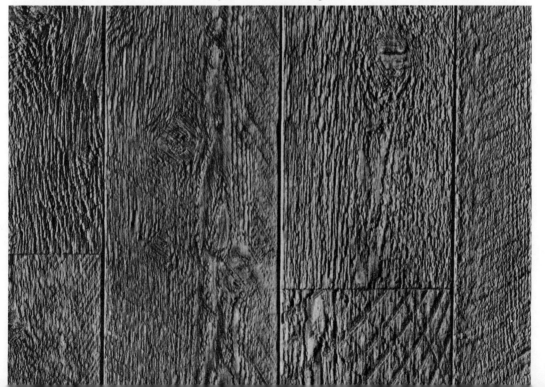

One of the standards in wall treatment is the big mural sold by paneling or lumber outlets. Patterns such as these by Marlite are in sheet form, ready for mounting on the wall. They are completely washable.

presses the pattern on the face of the sheet as it feeds through the machine. Since this process is simple, the variety of patterns and textures in hardboard is almost endless, and the cost factor is minimal.

Hardboard is also produced in a variety of prefinishes. Many of these are tough enough so they can be used as shower liners, and in other places demanding a moisture-resistant panel that is easily cleaned. And, through the right combination of texture and finish, hardboard can give you the look of stone, brick, or wood.

Another technique used for making hardboard sheets into simulations of natural materials is, actually, photographic. By a special printing process, a photographic copy of a rare and wonderful surface can be transmitted to a material that you put up in 4x8 sheets. The technique is also used to face sheets of particle board. A common method of achieving the pattern is lithography on a sheet of vinyl, which is laminated to the hardboard. The result is a perfect reproduction of the pattern—plus the durability and washability of sheet vinyl.

Plastic surfacing materials. These are what might be called "three dimensional wallpaper." Using wallpaper, you can paste up a *picture* of any wall surface, even one only available in antiquity. With a current group of vinyl plastic molded materials you can go a step further and reproduce the texture of the chosen surface as well as its color and tone. Companies like Decro-Wall mold bricks and stone and other materials into lifelike sheets (usually 12x24 or 24x24) that cement to the wall. What you end up with is a totally synthetic surface that is a perfect emulation of the kind of wall surfacing you could not afford in its original form.

These cement-on plastic surfaces are, of course, prefinished, and they are easy to maintain because of the washability of the plastic. They may, however, offer less resistance to physical damage than would be acceptable in heavy action areas or in areas of excessive heat.

Tile. This has long been an ideal material for walls that must take a beating—from heat, grease, water, steam, scrubbing. Ceramic tile is still popular today, in all of the traditional forms, plus many modern patterns and textures.

Moreover, one of the drawbacks of tile has been overcome. No longer is tiling a tedious square-by-tiny-square job. Your tile dealer can show you tiles unitized into larger elements that go up faster. Adhesives are improved, also. Once tile had to be set

One of the most recent entrees in the wall paneling market is molded plastic in patterns ranging from classic to ornate. The material comes in small (usually 2x2 feet or so) units that go on the wall with adhesives. Decro-Wall made this pattern.

Ceramic tile was once intended only for walls, but new, harder versions can go on floors when you want floors and walls to match exactly. The tile here, by Wenczel, is one of many different interfitting shapes.

in wet plaster. Then came mastics. Now there are silicone adhesives that are entirely waterproof, withstand normal household heat, and maintain a flexibility that keeps tile from working loose as changes in temperature cause changes in dimensions.

Tile these days is not always ceramic. You'll find good quality tiles made of plastic, duplicating most of the effects of ceramic, at much lower prices, and easier to install—but not equally resistant to wear

and damage. Also, the manufacturers of surfaced hardboard include excellent tile patterns in their lines, giving you tiling in sheet form, with the accompanying ease of installation. It performs excellently, even in such difficult areas as shower enclosures.

Fire-retardant materials. One highly specialized type of wall-surfacing material which may enter into your requirements is called "fire retardant." It comes in the form of a special ⅝-inch-thick gypsum board and also in plywood. Fire-retardant wood panels are manufactured with special adhesives that do not delaminate under heat. They may have mineral core—nonflammable—with wood veneer face as thin as one fortieth of an inch. Thus, even though the wood face may burn, it contributes relatively little to the fire. In addition, some fire-retardant plywood materials are produced on particle board or veneer cores that have been chemically treated for fire resistance. It is unlikely that your lumber or paneling dealer will carry fire-retardant plywood paneling, but if your situation requires the material, a list of manufacturers can be obtained from the American Wood Preservers Institute, 2600 Virginia Ave., Washington, D.C. 20037, or the Hardwood Plywood Manufacturers Association, 2310 S. Walter Reed Dr., Arlington, Va. 22206.

Other new or exceptional ideas for wall treatment include:

● The use on interior walls of materials intended for outdoors. Excellent and dramatic walls are being created with good old beveled siding. Homeowners who are lucky enough to find old barn siding are using it for paneling—particularly in family or activity rooms. Now and then you'll find, in magazines and papers specializing in antiques, entire paneled walls carefully stripped from an abandoned home, ready to be reassembled on your wall.

● Materials used in unorthodox ways. For example, the beveled siding mentioned above is sometimes applied vertically instead of horizontally. Others, intended for vertical use (such as wood-grain plywood or hardboard strip paneling) make interesting walls when they go up horizontally. Also, interesting, novel, and sometimes bizarre effects result from using such materials in checkerboard pattern, chevron pattern, or combinations of vertical and horizontal with lengths cut and applied at a 45-degree angle.

● Sometimes materials are mixed. Paneling is often combined with gypsum board, both in modern variations and in such classic applications as a wainscot of raised paneling. Extra interest on a plain wall can result from the application of molding in a pattern of horizontals, verticals, and rectangles, usually duplicating the effect of raised paneling.

Methods of handling most of these materials and methods will be covered in chapters that follow.

4

Gypsum Board

Virtually all smooth surface walls are plaster in one or the other of two forms. In older homes, regular plaster is most common. It is the material that is troweled on the wall in the form of a cementlike "mud" that dries into a smooth and hard finish. In newer homes, the plaster is preformed into rock-hard sheets backed and faced with tough paper. The sheets go on the wall with hammer and nails—or with adhesives—and the joints are concealed with a spacklelike material.

The sheet material is called gypsum board (because gypsum is the basic material of the plaster used in the sheets) or sheetrock. By any name, sheet-form plaster has given the homeowner a means of achieving a perfect base for paint or wallpaper, doing the job himself with typical handyman tools and no more than typical handyman skills. The job goes fast. You can do a wall in a weekend, including the paint job. Or, you can make it a bit-by-bit job, working at your own rate.

The materials are the sheets of gypsum board, special ringed nails that have extra holding power, tape you use to splice joints between sheets, a special plasterlike material that holds and covers the tape and also fills nail holes, and sometimes a special gun-fed mastic-adhesive, if you are using the adhesive method of application.

The tools are of the sort you most likely already have in your toolbox:

A standard 16-ounce nail hammer.

A knife of the type called "linoleum," intended for cutting with a down pressure pulling movement.

A gypsum board joint knife, which is like a spackling knife only somewhat wider.

A chisel or simply a butcher knife for smoothing off rough edges.

A mastic gun, if you are using the adhesive technique discussed below.

A nail set to sink nails when you apply trim.

A keyhole saw.

Since gypsum board is standard in sheets 4x8 feet, the dimension coincides with the standard 8-foot height of today's ceilings and the standard 4-foot module of today's wall stud spacing. That is what makes the job go fast. You stand a sheet up against the wall and nail it in place and 32 square feet of wall are surfaced.

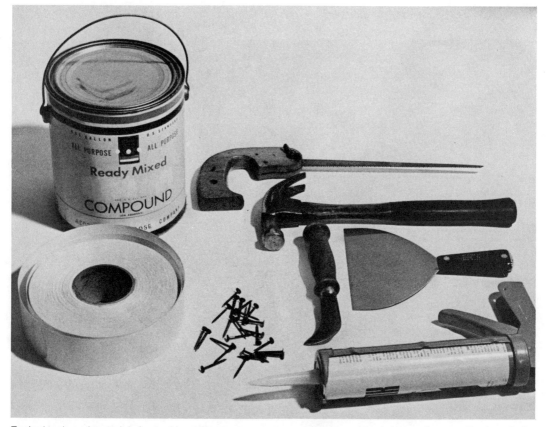

Typical tools and materials for working with gypsum: compound and tape, a keyhole saw, hammer, linoleum knife, joint knife, adhesive gun and tube, and special ringed nails.

Ringed nails intended for use with gypsum board hold harder, tend to eliminate nail popping.

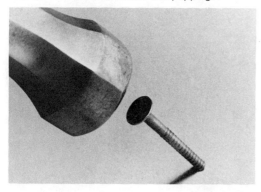

HANDLING THE FULL-SIZE SHEETS

The major problem most home handymen find while installing gypsum board is the somewhat cumbersome nature of the big sheets. They are fairly heavy, sometimes difficult to maneuver into position for nailing. A few simple steps, however, can make it a one-man job.

1. Put the bottom end of the sheet against the wall positioned as closely as possible to

How to Cut Gypsum Board

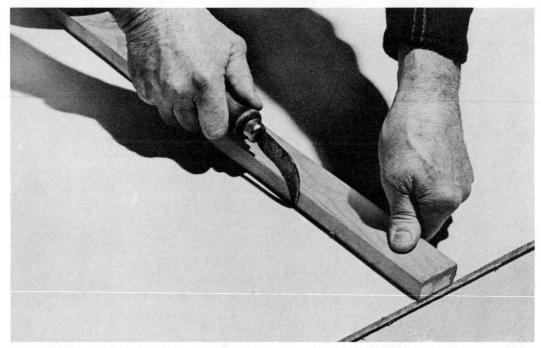

1. Place the sheet face up on a level surface. Position a straight length of 1x2 across it at the cutting point. Make two or three passes along the 1x2 with a linoleum or utility knife.

2. Slip the 1x2 under the sheet, on edge. When you apply pressure beside the 1x2, the sheet will break along the line you scored on the face.

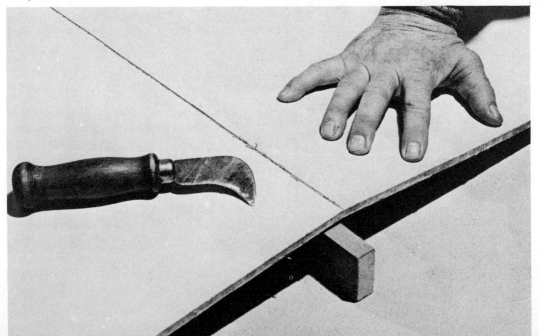

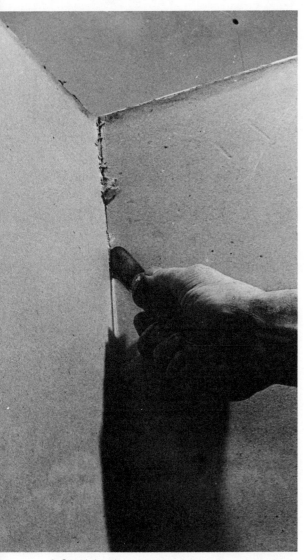

3. Stand the sheet on edge, bent at the cut as shown here. Run the knife along the back, to cut the backing paper.

its final lateral position. The face of the sheet goes face down on the floor.

2. Lift the end of the sheet and "walk" under it with your hands until it is in a vertical position.

3. Make any necessary lateral adjustments, then drive a nail through the center of the sheet at the top, into the 2x4 that runs across the top of the wall—the "plate."

This nail holds the sheet in position while you do the rest of the nailing.

Tricks for spacing and positioning. It is important not to fit sheets too tightly. Check the height of the wall. If it is slightly more than 8 feet, that is good. If it is less, each sheet must be cut off so that there is a space of about ¼-inch.

Laterally, you need a little space, too. One trick is to slip a nail between two sheets, to act as a spacer. This also allows the joint cement to work its way in, providing a tighter bond. Be sure to leave a little space at corners, too.

The space on the horizontal can be left at the top or the bottom depending on your plans for trim. If you will be using a picture mold between the wall and the ceiling, leave it at the top. It's easiest, and the picture mold will cover the space. However, if you plan a nonmolding joint at the ceiling, raise the sheet up to the top, using this technique.

1. Slip the end of a thin board under the bottom edge. Use a piece of ¼-inch plywood if the gap is small.

2. Slip a piece of 1x2 or 2x4 (depending on the space involved) under the board to act as a fulcrum.

3. Stand on the lever thus provided and let it hoist the sheet up into position while you nail it.

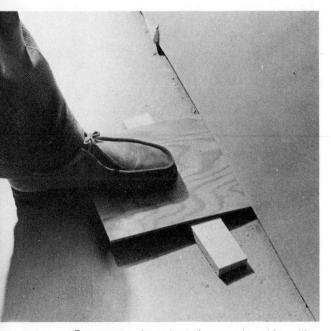

Easy way to raise a sheet of gypsum board for nailing tight against the ceiling is shown here. Slip a scrap of plywood under the edge, put a scrap of 1x2 under it to act as a fulcrum, and "lever" the sheet in place; then drive two or three nails to hold it.

A scrap of 1x2 nailed at the upper edge of a sheet acts as a support for the lower edge of the one above it, while you nail it in place.

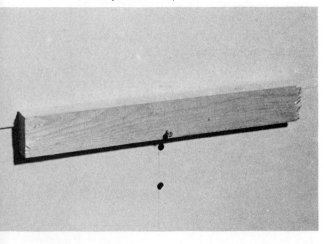

Walls over 8 feet high. In some older homes —and in some of the most modern— ceilings may run more than 8 feet. When the overage is slight, you may be able to put the space at the bottom, where it will be covered by the baseboard. If the ceiling height runs 9 feet or more, you can buy gypsum board 4x10 feet to accommodate the extra distance. If the wall is much more than 10 feet, and cannot be taken care of with 10-foot gypsum board, your best bet is to install 8-foot lengths, then cut pieces to take care of the difference. That way, you won't have to handle the cumbersome over-size sheets.

There are some methods and techniques that make the high wall job easier.

Dropped ceiling. This standard technique in high ceilinged rooms involves letting the ceiling treatment (for instance, paint) come down the wall for a foot or more. At that point, there is a molding. Below the molding is the wall treatment (for instance, wallpaper). The advantage of this when you put up gypsum board is that you can put the joint behind the molding, and not have the bother of taping and concealing it. You end up with 8 feet of wall treatment, the molding painted the same color as the ceiling or color picked up from the wallpaper, and the dropped ceiling. The only joints you have to take care of at the ceiling are the verticals—and they are easy, as you will see later on.

Wainscot or chair rail. Another method of handling the high ceiling is to put up a wall of gypsum board, with a chair rail or a wainscot at the bottom. A chair rail is a flat molding, usually 3 or 4 inches wide, nailed horizontally along the wall. The standard height is about 3 feet, although it can be higher or lower if you wish. (The basic, and original, purpose of the chair rail is to prevent damage to the wall where backs of chairs hit it.) Most often, the wall below a chair rail is painted and the wall above papered. Or, it may be painted a different color. The chair rail itself can be white or some color that goes with the decor.

The wainscot is actual paneling along the bottom 3 feet or so of the wall. It is discussed in a later chapter.

If you adopt the chair-rail method of handling a high wall, follow these steps:

1. First, cut pieces of gypsum board the *height of the middle* of the chair rail. Nail them in place.

2. Nail temporarily a piece of 1x2 along the top of this row of sheets so that it laps over the top a half inch or so. This forms a groove or channel along the top.

3. Position the bottom edge of the larger pieces of sheet on the 1x2. Lift the other end and "walk" it up. The bottom will slip into the groove, firmly in place until you get it nailed. Then remove the 1x2.

4. Treat the vertical joints and the joint at the ceiling. The chair rail will cover the horizontal joint.

The same basic technique works with the wainscot. Install it first, then let the top of the paneling act as the support while you walk the sheets into place and nail them. End up with the molding at the top of the wainscot, covering the raw bottom ends of the sheets.

If your decision is to let the wall be plain, regardless of height, you must make this decision: does the joint go up near the ceiling or does it go down below? Here are some factors in that decision:

● End joints are difficult to make absolutely invisible, so you might want to put the joints up high—where they may not be so noticeable.

● Sometimes the arrangement of furni-

If ceiling exceeds 8 feet in height, one method of filling the space is by installing wainscot at the bottom. The wainscot shown here consists of raised panels, described in Chapter 10.

ture, etc., along a wall will conceal the joint, if it is at the lower level.

● It is easier to stand full sheets up and nail them; then, put the smaller, lighter pieces above them.

● On the other hand, the 1x2 trick mentioned above can be used, if you decide to put the joint down low.

Lateral positioning. It is to be assumed that the wall studs are spaced to give you a vertical every 48 inches. However, because of corner construction and because the wall itself may not be a convenient complement of 48 inches, it may be necessary for you to do some figuring to keep work at a minimum.

First, measure from a corner out to the stud that should be at 48 inches. If it isn't, try the other corner. If it gives you the proper spacing, start in that corner and work to the other. At that corner, you'll have to cut a strip to fit. Put the cut edge in the corner. If neither corner gives you 48-inch spacing, start one stud from the corner. Work across the wall. Now cut a sheet vertically to fill the spaces at the corners.

HOW TO NAIL GYPSUM BOARD IN PLACE

Gypsum board installation requires careful nailing and certain special techniques. In the first place, you must not expect the nails to pull the sheet up tight against the studs. Instead, you must apply enough pressure to hold the sheet up tight, then drive the nail. This is because of the relatively delicate nature of the sheet; it is easy to rupture with the hammer if it is not backed up properly.

Secondly, you must be careful to avoid hammering the nail too far into the board. Be certain not to drive it so far that the surface paper is broken. If you do, you ruin the holding power of that nail. When that happens, drive another nail a couple of inches from the first—this time making sure that you don't drive it too far.

On the other hand, each nail should be driven far enough so that the surface is "dimpled." This is important, since you need the "dimple" to accept the dab of joint compound that conceals the nail. If the nail head protrudes even slightly above the surface, it is virtually impossible to conceal it.

One of the problems with gypsum board is called "nail popping." Changes in temperature and humidity cause the nails to

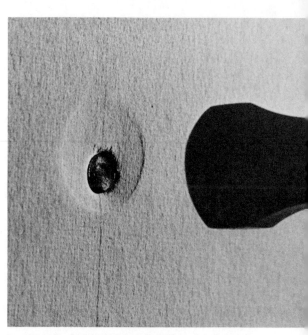

Proper nailing sinks the head of the nail just barely into the surface of the gypsum board, leaving a "dimple" which you fill later, concealing the nail.

When the nail is not "dimpled" the knife strikes the head, and leaves an unsightly ridge like this.

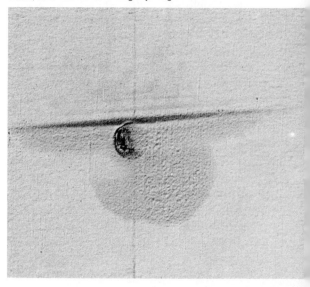

work out, breaking the compound that covered them. To minimize the chances that this will happen, you might want to adopt the *double-nail technique* now used by many professionals. They drive the first nail, then drive another about 2 inches away from it. This gives double holding power, and since the two nails are so close together there is no additional labor involved in knifing the compound over them.

Important: Nails should be driven about 6 inches apart along the edges of the sheet and about every 12 inches along the studs in the "field" of the sheet. This spacing applies both to double and to single nailing. Be sure to use the special ringed nails designed specifically for holding power in gypsum board installation.

MASTIC-ADHESIVE APPLICATION

There is an increasing trend toward the use of adhesives in the application of gypsum board. With this system, you use a special adhesive and an applicator; building supply dealers sell these. With the applicator, run a squiggle of adhesive along the studs. The bead should be about ⅜-inch in diameter.

Then, place the sheets in position and nail them only at the edges. The adhesive does the job along the studs that run back of the sheets.

You can make the adhesive technique even more effective with this trick: Put two 2x4s on edge a little less than 8 feet apart on the floor. Lay the sheets face up with the ends resting on these 2x4s. Leave them that way for a day or so. This causes the sheets to take on a curve. Then, when you nail them at the ends, the curve makes them hug the studs, and adhesion is more certain. With this technique nailing is held to a minimum, and joint treatment is therefore

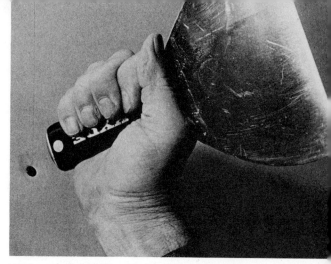

Hardware stores carry special joint knives with a "hammer handle" you can use to sink a nail a little further when it happens to be too far above surface.

When you use a mastic-adhesive to apply gypsum board, you eliminate much nailing and patching. This photo shows the "squiggle" of adhesive.

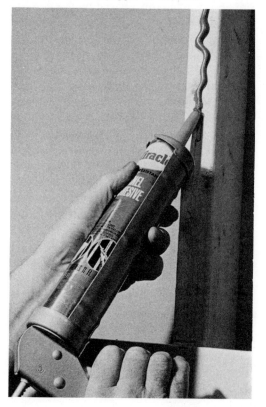

much easier. Perhaps more important, nail popping is almost surely eliminated.

HOW TO HIDE JOINTS AND NAILS

While the application of sheets is almost pure carpentry, treating joints and nail heads is closer to pure artistry. And there are no workable shortcuts.

You can buy joint cement either in the form of a powder that you mix with water, or in gallon cans already mixed. Either way, the application techniques are the same, although the ready-mixed material saves time and work for the home handyman. At the same time, it guarantees you a proper mixture.

The joint tape comes in rolls. Your dealer can tell you whether you need a small roll or two—or a big roll—based on the number of sheets you buy. (He'll also estimate for you how many pounds you'll need of the special ringed nails you should use.)

Joint treatment involves these steps:

1. Using the wide blade joint knife, "butter" the joint between two sheets. You'll note that the edges are slightly thinner than the rest of the sheet. This provides a "valley" into which the joint treatment is troweled.

2. Immediately, lay a strip of tape in the wet compound, and use the knife to smooth it down. Pick up the excess that oozes out at the sides and trowel it on top of the tape. Work to be sure the tape is smooth. This may require lifting it and troweling it down a second time, since the tape expands when it is wet. (It may help to dampen the strip of tape four or five minutes in advance, so that the elongation takes place before you trowel the tape into the compound.)

3. Work the knife repeatedly along the joint until you have spread the compound smoothly. Pick up the excess and return it to the mix container.

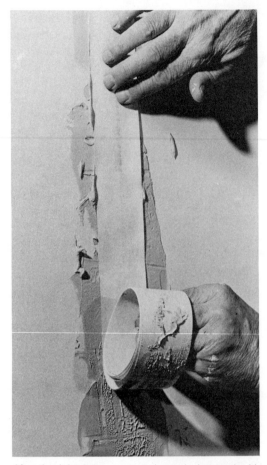

After the joint between two sheets is buttered with joint cement, smooth joint tape into the cement, carefully centered over the crack.

4. Let this application dry. Then use fine sandpaper on an 8-inch long piece of 2x4 or 1x4 to sand off any roughness and high spots, holding the sanding block so that it bridges the valley. It is possible to remove slight roughness without the dust and cleanup problems of sanding. Wrap a piece of wet toweling around a 2x4 or 1x4 block and rub it in long, smooth strokes over the dried joint. The moisture softens the high spots, smoothing them down to the proper level.

Since this technique is most effective on

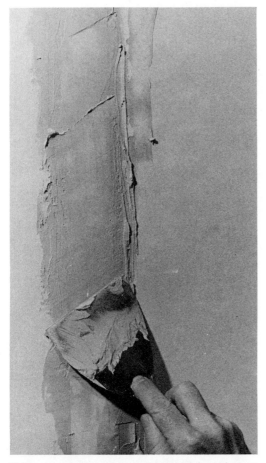

Using excess cement from the initial buttering, or more cement from the mix, cover the tape completely. The ideal taping job has the tape buried in the cement after it has been smoothed.

Second coatings of the joint compound must be "skived" out to a feather edge on both sides of the initial tape application.

Key to a smooth joint is a good-size sandpaper block that will bridge gaps and smooth off high spots.

relatively fine, "toothy" roughness, you may have to finish up with coarse sandpaper when the joint cement is more wavy then toothy.

5. Now add a small amount of water to the standard joint compound mix, to make it slightly thinner. Carefully trowel this thinner mixture over the dried and sanded area, bringing it up to level smoothness. Allow to dry and sand carefully.

It may be necessary to repeat this last

Properly dimpled nail gives this result with the first application of compound. Subsequent applications make the wall perfectly smooth.

step, depending on the roughness of the first application, and on the amount of practice you've had at gypsum board joint treatment.

Covering nails. You'll use a similar two coat application to cover nails in the middle of the sheet.

1. Trowel a dab of compound over the nail head, making it as smooth as possible. When it is dry, sand it. Be careful not to abrade the paper around the nail unnecessarily, since this may cause roughness in the final finish.

2. Using a spackling motion of the knife, fill the slight depression that will occur because of contraction when the compound dries.

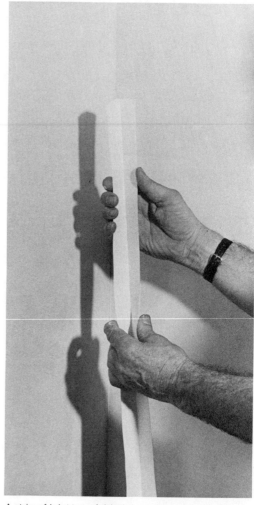

A strip of joint tape folded down the center fits into inside corners after they are buttered.

Covering end joints. Since there is no thinness at the ends of the sheets providing a "valley" in which to bury the joint treatment, you use a technique similar to the nail-covering method. However, when you apply the second coat, you must "skive" it out on either side in a gentle slope that minimizes the ridge caused by the first application.

Special corner reinforcement comes from a metal angle-strip. It is more rugged than a corner that is merely taped.

When you apply compound to the corner, the bead of the metal reinforcement strip serves as a knife guide.

Covering corner joints. The first step in filling an inside corner is to butter both surfaces. Then, cut a strip of tape the right length and fold it down the middle, lengthwise. Put this bent strip in the corner and work it into position with the joint knife, stroking downward first along one wall, then the other. Let this application dry, sand it, then smooth on a finish coat.

Outside corners can be done by bending a strip of tape around the corner, in a reverse of the inside corner. But, there is a better way; your dealer can sell you a metal corner strip that you nail in place. It is in the form of two perforated flanges that fit along the walls, plus a bead that forms the exact corner. You use this bead as a guide for one side of the knife when you trowel on the joint compound. Smooth it out along both walls. Sand and recoat. This metal corner not only makes a neater and easier job, but protects the corner from damage.

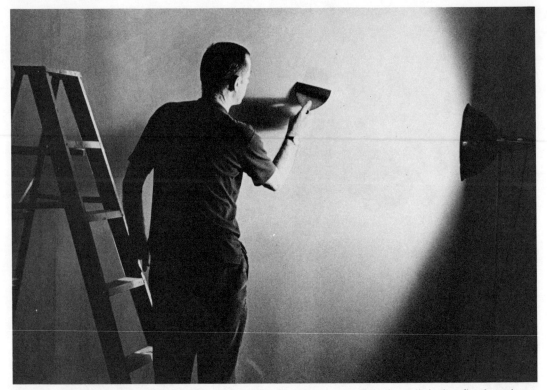

You can make it easier to spot irregularities that must be filled if you cross-light the wall. A photoflood, as shown here, is ideal for the task.

WHAT ABOUT ELECTRICAL OUTLETS?

If your installation of gypsum board covers an area where there are electrical outlets or switches, you must cut holes in the material before you nail it up. Measure carefully to establish the location. Pencil mark the holes just slightly larger than the boxes, so that the sheet will slip around them. A keyhole saw works best. Just jab it through the sheet in the middle of the rec-tangle where the hole is to be. Then cut along the lines. Ordinarily, you will be able to shove the sheet past the little "ears" that accept cover plate screws at the top and bottom of the box.

Important: If you install the electrical boxes yourself, be sure that they extend $3/8$ or $1/2$ an inch out from the front edge of the stud, depending on the thickness of the gypsum board you're using.

5

Paint: The Most Popular Wall Surface

The most popular wall-surfacing material is paint. Painting is the home handyman's ideal project—it's easy, whether you brush on the paint or use a speedy roller. It's quick, because modern latex paints are ready for recoating in hours and some cover so well that you never need a second coat. And it's cheap, compared to any other method of making a wall attractive and functional.

Modern paint formulas can take care of just about any possible protective requirement you may have. Water resistance and washability are improved. A special formula can even provide fire resistance. The paint turns to foam when heated, forming insulation that helps protect the wall behind it from catching fire. It's called "intumescent." Although this paint isn't available from every neighborhood hardware store paint department, it is worth shopping for if you want extra protection—for example around a child's room.

In addition, many situations demand paint and won't tolerate anything else. An obvious example is trim. Another is an old rough plastered wall with so many hills and hollows that wallpaper can't follow the contours. Also, when the decision is made to change the appearance of a masonry wall, the only solution aside from paneling is paint.

WHICH PAINT GOES WHERE?

Paint technology has reached a point where, today, you can use one of the so-called "latex paints" just about anywhere. No longer are they reserved for areas where there is little exposure to dirt, moisture, and other damage. They are just as washable as oil-base paints. In fact, some paint manufacturers are now out with latex

39

enamels that are recommended for outdoor furniture.

This means, of course, that you no longer have to think in terms of latex paints for walls and oil base enamels for trim. Gone are the days when you bought a flat paint for the walls and a glossy paint for trim. Semigloss trim paints are completely washable.

And, some lines of flat wall paint are absolutely scrubbable without loss of color or surface sheen. This degree of easy maintenance will sooner or later go into every paint can. As of now, it is a good idea to check manufacturers' labels and literature, to see how they rate their wall and trim paints. Some of the latest formulas include Teflon-E, a special version of the well-known easy-wash material. Mixed into a paint, it gives the wall a washability almost equal to a Teflon coated frying pan's.

Here is a basic round-up of indoor paints:

Latex paint. The word "latex" originally stemmed from the use of rubber in one form or another as the resin—or solid—in the paint. The solvent, or thinner—or "vehicle" as it is sometimes called—was water. Today, many paints are being made with water as the thinner but with resins that are not latex, and the industry is leaning toward such terms as "water-thinned" or "water-reducible." If the paints are called latex at all, the term often used is "acrylic latex," an acrylic resin being the body of the paint. Actually, the term "latex" in this case is a carry over from the rubber-base days, since the acrylic is a resin, not a latex. Nevertheless, the term persists.

In addition to the speed of drying and new opacity and washability of acrylic latex paints, the greatest advantage of water-thinnables is water clean-up. The expense —and the potential fire damage—of volatile thinners and brush cleaners is gone. If you wash the brush immediately after the session is over, it comes clean in a few minutes.

And, water clean-up is even more important when you apply paint with a roller, backed up by a brush for tight spots, because the time and material saved are even greater.

Alkyd resin paints. The use of the synthetic alkyd resin for solvent-thinned (oil-base) paints has brought several advantages. One of the most useful is a special formulation that makes the paint yogurt-thick. A brush dipped in it carries many times as much paint to the surface. Yet, under the friction of stroking, the paint spreads and smooths readily.

In standard forms—gloss and satin— alkyd materials are still preferred by many for trim, doors, even heavy traffic hallways. Many homeowners still like them best for bathrooms and kitchens, where they feel more confident of washability despite the availability of water-thinned enamels in satin or gloss, guaranteed to clean up with standard household cleaning materials.

The opacity of paints—their ability to cover completely one color with another— has been improved through the addition of an entirely new ingredient. When the paint is manufactured, a portion of the white pigment particles (titanium dioxide) is replaced with a material that diffuses and evaporates, leaving minute tiny bubbles. These "microvoids" reflect and scatter light, giving the paint the effect of more thickness than it really has. With paints of this formula, one coat of white will cover black completely. A greater tribute to opacity in the eyes of many paint experts, it will cover bright yellow.

You may be interested, also, in an unusual paint that looks dead flat when viewed head on, but takes on a soft luster when you look at it from an angle.

Textured-surface paints. One of the most interesting of wall treatments in certain situations is textured paint. The degree and type of texturing varies. In one form, it comes from nothing more than tiny sandlike particles suspended in the paint that give the wall a sand textured look. It is often used over smooth gypsum board when you want an old, colonial look to go with early American surroundings. You can buy paint with the granules already in it. Or, you can buy the granules (minute glass beads) and stir them into ordinary paint. If you choose the mix-it-yourself method, your choice of colors is unlimited—although the sandy texture is most often used with white or quite light colors.

Another form of texture paint is thick bodied, and you texture it after it is on the wall. Special tools are available for texturing, or you can use a sponge, a wadded paper towel, or any other improvisation that gives you the results you want. Some homeowners do the texturing with a basic texture paint, then brush on the final color with regular paint. One drawback with the deeply textured versions is that you can't get back easily to a smooth wall if you decide later on that you have had enough of the textured look.

Masonry paint. While most of the water thinned paints (check the labels) can be used over brick, concrete, concrete block, or other masonry walls, there are times when the special features of cementitious paints are ideal. The paints, made by stirring a cement powder into water, are pancake batter thick. As you brush them on masonry surfaces, they tend to fill the depressions, reducing the amount of texture. In many cases the paint even obscures the mortar courses in concrete block construction, producing a wall that is uniform in texture. The cementitious paints can be tinted with special colorants sold by masonry supply outlets. Also, you can paint over them with regular latex paints. The result is a relatively smooth masonry wall, any color you want it. A common brand name is Thoroseal.

Varnish. Very little varnish is used on walls, except on paneled walls, and its application there is covered in the section on paneling. The clear finish, however, is still sometimes used on trim, as it once was almost universally. If you happen to live in a very old house that still has varnished trim, the varnish is no doubt badly cracked and crazed. The best bet might be to paint it this time around. Working on a new surface with varnish, you do the job fastest with a prime coat of shellac, followed by a coat or two of varnish.

Varnishes, like paints and enamels, have undergone great changes lately. The most popular and most durable these days are those made with urethane resins (check labels), and there are even clear water-thinnable finishes available from some manufacturers.

Primers. When you paint over a clean painted wall, no primer is required. When you paint over plaster or gypsum board, a primer prepares the surface. With some paints, unpainted plaster causes trouble because of its alkaline nature. On gypsum board, the primer prevents undue penetration of the paint into the paper surface of the sheets.

Although you can paint over wallpaper with latex paints, it is sometimes necessary to start with a prime coat, to prevent the pigments in the wallpaper pattern from softening and "bleeding" into the paint. Check it out by painting a small area.

Since various paint products and various paint brands have varying specifications regarding primers, it is best to confer with your dealer about the specific paint you are buying. Often you will be able to tint the primer toward the final color, using it not only to prime the surface but as the first coat of the paint job. Some primers are latex — quick to dry. They don't add much in time consumed. This is true also of primers based on shellac.

HOW MUCH PAINT DO YOU NEED?

Typically, a gallon of paint will cover 450 square feet. It is important to realize that when the manufacturer says on the label that it will cover 450 square feet, *he doesn't want you to stretch it beyond that.* If you do, you sacrifice total overall performance. In fact, if you ask a gallon to cover only 400 square feet, you may be doing yourself a favor.

To determine the amount of paint required to cover a wall, multiply the height of the wall by its length, then divide by 400. That means a gallon of paint would cover a room 10 by 15 feet, one coat. Two coats would take two gallons. However, there are other factors.

When a wall is textured, or rough-troweled, it takes more paint than a smooth wall. This is because the texture represents *added surface to be covered,* even though it does not contribute to the size of the area. It is impossible to suggest the additional amount of paint a textured wall requires, but it could be as much as 50 percent more.

Most walls have doors or windows or other areas that are not painted. If the non-paint area is small — say a single window or door — ignore it. However, two or three windows, a door and a window, multiple sliding doors, a large fireplace, these offer a little saving in materials, if not in labor. As the accompanying diagram shows, you can subtract the area of the openings. (Meanwhile, the ceiling must be figured at length times width of the room.)

Using these figures and the current price of paint in your area, you can estimate the cost of doing over a room. Add to the cost for wall paint the cost of a couple of quarts of trim paint.

Important: The only trim areas of a house that may really need special trim paint are the windows. More and more, today's homeowners and professional painters are using wall paint for the trim that is not exposed to freezing, heating, and condensation. This is most convenient when the trim and the wall are the same color.

WHAT ABOUT THE COLOR?

No book can tell you which colors you like best. If you want a pale purple wall with pea-green polka dots, go ahead. But knowing some facts about colors may help you in deciding.

White reflects the most light of any color. This makes it a logical choice in a room that is served by a relatively small window area. White is often used on the side of a room opposite the windows, even though other walls may be papered or painted in less reflective colors. The white wall reflects light back into the room.

Greens are the most restful colors, no doubt because green is the color we see most often in nature. This makes green appropriate for any room in the house — but most appropriate for a room where peace

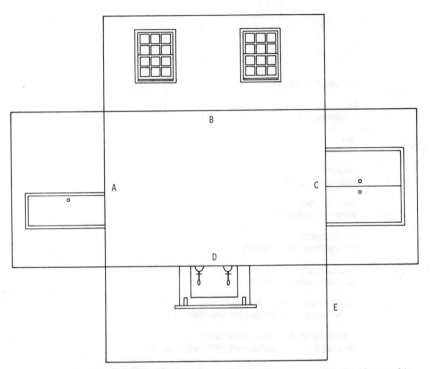

This schematic drawing of a room with the walls laid flat gives you several items of information about paint quantities.

To determine quantities, add the width of A, B, C, and
D and multiply by E—the height.

To find floor or ceiling area, multiply A by B.

To find the area of any wall, multiply its width by E.

If a wall has only a door (A) or other small opening (D)
ignore it in your area figures.

If a wall has a large opening (C) or several windows (B),
subtract their area from the wall total. One window is
not a factor, unless the wall is quite small.

and quiet are the basic objectives.

Red is the noisiest, the most exciting color. Most experts in color and decor use it sparingly, only as accents.

Orange is the most visible of all colors, which is the reason for recent changes from red to bright orange for fire fighting equipment in many communities. Where does it fit into the home? It might be the ideal color for a railing down a dark basement stairway.

Blue is the cool color. Many decorators recommend it for the rooms on the sunny side of the house, and at the same time recommend colors on the warm side of the spectrum for rooms with northern or eastern exposure.

Yellow is a warm cheerful color. Reflectance is second only to white, making it a good color for use in poorly lighted rooms, hallways, stairways.

Violet and purple are cool colors, both a

COLOR   PERCENTAGE OF LIGHT REFLECTANCY

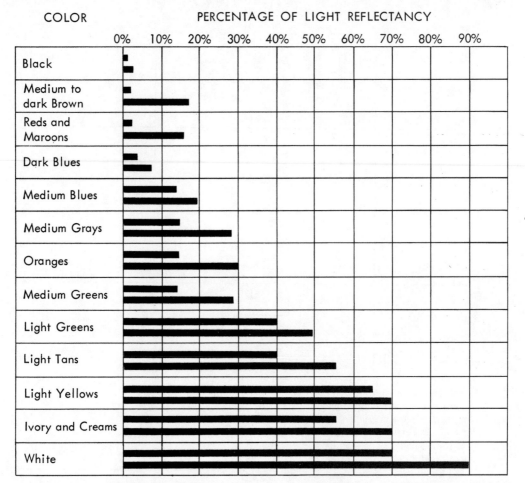

The amount of light reflected (reflectancy) by various colors is given in this chart. The variation of reflectancy for each color is determined mainly by the surface texture. For example, a flat surface reflects less light than one that is glossy.

little intense for most tastes. Yet, toned down to lavender, purple becomes a dignified hue — perhaps a little too aloof.

Gray is the the no color color. It is completely neutral, and can therefore be considered the ideal background color. You might like it in a room where furnishings themselves are bright and colorful, as the background color for a wall of shelves on which lively colored objects are displayed.

Used this way, gray occupies the same role as "off white," which is usually slightly warmer than gray.

Which colors go where? Just as it is impossible to delineate which colors are best for each individual, so is it impossible to lay down rules about colors for the different rooms in the house. Color experts, however, suggest that some colors are more ap-

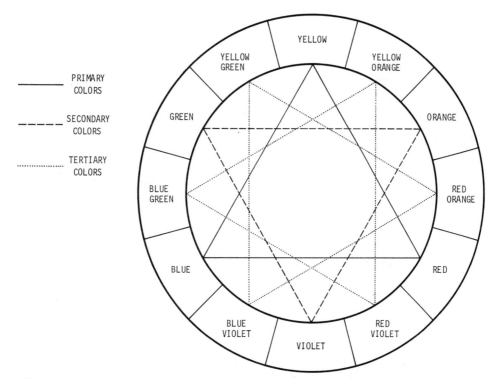

PRIMARY COLORS

SECONDARY COLORS

TERTIARY COLORS

This is the "color wheel," showing how combinations of colors produce other colors or tints. Combining two primary colors produces a secondary color. The tertiaries result from mixtures that are not even. For example, red and yellow make orange. Two parts of red and one of yellow make red-orange. Two parts of yellow and one red make yellow-orange.

propriate for certain rooms than for others. Their recommendations, of course, must be modified by personal tastes.

Living rooms tend toward more activity when they are painted warm colors. With walls of cool colors, the room is more quiet, more restful.

Dining rooms are best, the experts say, in "food" colors. Greens, light browns, yellows, peach, rose, and the like are colors that stimulate the appetite. They make the food look attractive. They are good dining companions.

Bedrooms are, more than any other room in the house, the private rooms of the indi-

viduals. Therefore, why not have them the color the occupant likes best? Young people seem to perfer warm colors in their bedrooms. Older folks lean toward neutral colors. Experts advise against too much brightness in color and too much action in patterns in bedrooms. The recommendation for sickrooms is blue.

Color and the size of the room. The color you pick for the walls of a room should take one more factor into consideration: the size of the room. These are the points to remember.

● Warm colors make a room seem

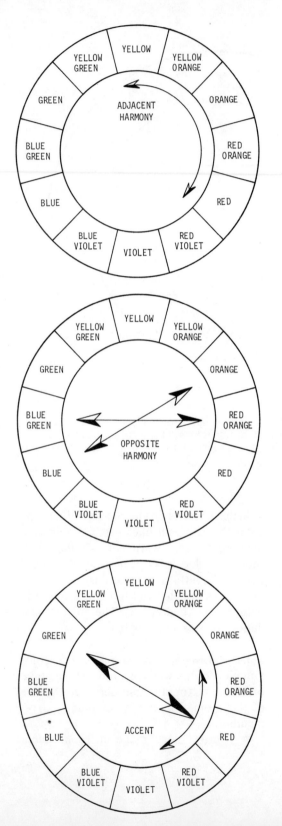

Colors that are next to each other on the color wheel produce the "gentlest" harmony, low in contrast and conservative in overall effect.

Colors that are opposite each other on the wheel produce the most drastic contrasts — strong, dramatic, often too much so for use in areas of the home where calmness is important.

Common method of achieving accent in decorating colors is to let adjacent colors cover the majority of the room, with a color from the opposite side of the wheel as the accent.

smaller. The reason for this is that warm colored things always *seem closer to you.*

● Cool colors make rooms seem larger, because cool colored things always seem farther away.

● Patterns and shapes make a room seem smaller.

● Smooth textures and patternless walls seem farther away.

These factors can also be used to change a seeming shape of a room. For instance, if the room is long and narrow, you can "bring the far wall closer" by giving it a warm color or pattern or both. Conversely, you can "send the close wall farther away" by giving it an even, cool color.

Mixing color. You can get paint any color you want it, owing to modern custom-mix processes. Have it done at the store, or buy the base color and some tubes of pigment that paint stores sell. There are some precautions, when you buy paint of any mixed color.

● Be sure you buy enough. In spite of the careful mechanics of custom mixing, it is not uncommon for the second gallon you buy to be noticeably different from the first gallon. And, if you go back a year later, the difference may be tremendous.

● If you buy more than one gallon, it may be wise to intermix them, pouring both gallons into a larger pail, then stirring them thoroughly before you return them to the cans with lids. Professionals often do this, because they know that there can be slight differences, can to can. The reason for this is the extreme intensity of the added pigments. Only a minute difference in quantities of pigments can make a difference the eye won't tolerate.

6

Preparing Walls for Paint

Whether a wall is new or being repainted, chances are it needs some preparation. The success of a paint job depends as much on the "substrate" it goes over as it does on the materials and methods used in applying it. The new wall normally needs only priming. It is also a good idea to make one last examination of gypsum-board applications, to be sure all the joint treatments are sanded smooth and any depressions are filled. These defects often show up more prominently after a wall is painted than they do in the raw.

Dirt. If a wall is only slightly soiled, with normal household accumulations—mostly from particles circulating in the air—it may be possible to ignore the dirt and go ahead and paint. Large accumulations, however, should be cleaned away. Sometimes brisk brooming will do the job, removing dust and dirt that may have been out of sight or out of reach during normal housecleaning procedures.

Oily dirt. This must come off the wall. It is most common, of course, in kitchens, but in houses where the kitchen is part of another area, such as the common kitchen-dining area, the grease from cooking usually spreads to the nonkitchen walls.

The basic trick in cleaning a dirty wall is to go at the job almost as though you were cleaning a dirty floor. Don't depend on "easy does it" cleaning products in spray cans, and the like. These may leave a surface that is no more friendly to the paint than the dirt would have been. Pick up a sponge-type floor mop, with a squeeze handle. Mix a pail full of warm water with a couple of tablespoons of detergent—the type meant for automatic dishwashers. (The basis of these detergents is trisodium phosphate, and you may be able to buy it cheaper as TSP in a paint store than as a dishwashing detergent in the supermarket.) Follow these steps:

1. With the sponge just slightly less than dripping wet, go over a vertical strip of the wall about 2 feet wide.

2. Squeegee the dirty water out of the sponge into a different pail, or down the drain.

3. Go over the wall with the squeezed

sponge, to pick up as much of the remaining dirty water as possible.

4. Rinse the sponge in clean water, and go over the area again, to rinse and remove the rest of the dirt and detergent-treated water.

5. Move on to the next strip.

This routine sounds tedious, but actually it goes fast, and you end up with a wall that is clean and ready to accept paint that won't peel off.

Defective paint. If the walls you are about to paint show defects in the existing paint, such as peeling, crazing, or flaking, your first move should be to try to determine what caused the defects in the first place. Will the same thing happen to the paint you are about to put on?

Check for moisture conditions, excessive heat, and improper previous techniques. Are there many coats of paint on the wall, producing a build-up that cannot tolerate expansion and contraction due to temperature change?

If the cause of failure can be determined and corrected, try your hand at sanding the edges of the deteriorated areas, making them blend into the okay area so that they won't show when the new paint goes on. If you can't do this, or if the amount of deterioration is excessive, your solution may have to be wallpapering or paneling. Or, a badly roughened existing wall may be the real excuse for going for a textured wall surface.

High gloss paint. It is frequently bad practice to attempt to put a new paint job over a substrate that is highly glossy. This is because part of the adhesion of paint comes from the way it "interlocks" with the old surface. Flat or semigloss surfaces usually provide enough "tooth" so that the new

paint adheres well. A glossy substrate paint may let go of the new paint almost as soon as it has hardened. This is most likely if there is even a trace of oiliness on the gloss.

The solution is a washdown with strong trisodium phosphate. Use the sponge-type floor mop mentioned above, but work in a saturated solution of TSP. Mix the powder in hot water until no more will dissolve. Swab it on the wall, sponge it dry, rinse with a sponge full of clear, fresh water. Sponge dry. Rinse a second time. The strong chemical action of the TSP will cut the gloss off the old paint, leaving you with a good substrate.

Wallpaper. Wallpaper that is soundly adhering and smooth is an acceptable substrate for wall paint. However, if it does not adhere tightly to the wall, any paint you put on it will peel off with the wallpaper. There is also the unpleasant look of paint over lapped joints in wallpaper. The joints show through the paint like conspicuous ribbons stretched floor to ceiling.

Unless wallpaper is sound and smooth and nonbleeding, you will save time and aspirin by removing it entirely. Rent a steamer that will make the old paper fall off in festoons. Or, ask the paint dealer for a wallpaper remover. This is a "surface tension reducer" that makes water wetter, so it will soak through the paper and soften the adhesive beneath it. Removing paper by any means is messy, but it is the only perfect answer when you want to convert a papered wall to a painted wall.

CRACKED OR DAMAGED WALLS

Some homeowners are lucky enough to live in a house so well built that the walls never show any cracks or other structural defects. But in most houses, settling and

Examples of patching materials excellently suited for cracks in plaster or gypsum board. Plaster of paris in bags is the most economical when the repairs involve filling large voids.

shifting (so subtle you'd never notice it) produces strains on the wall surfacing material that result in cracks ranging from hairline to serious. In some houses, the faulting repeats every year, with changes in temperature, heating, and humidity.

The degree of cracking and fissuring in walls is usually greater with plaster than it is with gypsum board, because the tough paper surfacing of the sheet material helps support the natural brittleness of plaster. Gypsum board failures are most likely to be in the joints, or where nails pop. (Nail popping is the biggest reason why the use of adhesives is wise when you install gypsum board.)

Patching cracks in plaster involves these steps:

● Select a premixed patching com-pound, or one that you mix with water. The joint compound intended for gypsum board works well and is easy to handle. If, however, the cracks are big and extensive, you may want to save money by using plaster of Paris to do the initial, bulky filling. Then switch to a ready mixed filler for the final touch-up.

● Use a wide spackle knife to apply the filler, working to force the patching material deep into the crack. You may find it easier to drive the material deep if you make the initial application by "buttering" it on with a cross-crack motion of the knife. Then switch to a with-the-crack motion. When the crack is filled, smooth it as carefully as possible.

If you are patching a sand textured surface, the patching material will tend to fill in

To mix a batch of plaster, estimate the amount needed, then put enough water in a mixing pan to equal that amount. Sprinkle powder over the water and stir until the mix is the right thickness.

Remove switch plates and outlet plates and lay them out on newspapers to be painted. Return the screws loosely to the fixture and dab a bit of paint on them, so they'll match.

around the sand particles, leaving the areas smoother than the rest of the wall. Avoid this by mopping up the filler that flanks the patch, so the texture remains unfilled. Deposit sand over the remaining smooth area of the patch.

If the surface being patched is smooth, you must be careful not to make the patch conspicuous by *giving* it a texture. To avoid any kind of textured look around the patch, use a damp towel to wipe off all the patching material flanking the crack on both sides.

● On the other hand, if the surface is deliberately textured, and if the crack is very wide, you may have to resort to some intaglio sculpturing to produce a surface that will blend into its surroundings when it is painted. This operation will be easiest if you do it after the patch has started to harden, but before it sets completely. Use whatever tools will make the textures you want—anything from a pocket comb to a lead pencil to a butcher knife.

Patching holes in gypsum board. While a plastered wall may be more likely to present problems with cracks, a gypsum board wall may be more likely to present you with problems of patching through-the-surface holes. It is not unusual that some sharp cornered piece of furniture is accidently rammed against the wall, puncturing the sheet material.

Repairing such damage takes a little time, but it can be done with simple tools and techniques.

If the hole is quite large, the method of repair involves these steps.

1. With a keyhole or other saw, cut horizontally from the top and the bottom of the hole to the stud on both sides.

2. Use a sharp knife to cut down the center of each stud, from the top cross cut to the lower.

3. Remove the rectangle of gypsum board. This provides you with a "seat" on both sides, for an inset of the sheet material. Be sure that the seats are clean and free of dirt, nails, or chips of plaster.

4. Cut a piece of board of the same thickness to fit the opening. Nail it in place.

5. Use standard gypsum board joint treatments to complete the patch.

If the hole is relatively small, patching it involves only one problem; there isn't any

back-up for patching material. You can make a bottom, using the instructions that follow.

1. Cut the hole into a roughly rectangular shape, keeping it as small as possible.

2. Cut a scrap of gypsum board about 4 inches bigger than the hole in both directions. Punch two holes near the center of this piece of sheet, and tie a loop of fairly strong cord through the two holes.

3. Butter ready-mixed patching material on the face of the piece of gypsum board, at the edges.

4. Slip the piece through the hole on the diagonal, maneuver it around into position, then pull it forward so that the smear of patching material comes into contact with the back of the gypsum board around the hole.

5. Pull the string tight and tie it around a scrap of 1x2 or similar stock positioned across the hole.

When the patching cement hardens, it will hold the piece of sheet to the back side of the hole. Cut off the string. Now all you have to do is trowel patching material into the depression, which is only as deep as the existing wall material is thick. It will take two or three applications.

To save patching cement, if you happen to have enough scraps of the gypsum board around, you can cut a piece to fit in the depression. Butter the back with cement. *Gently* press it against the back-up piece. Then, use the standard crack patching techniques to fill the rectangle of crack around the patch.

Repairing extensive damage. If you should find it necessary to repair a large area of the wall—perhaps after flooding or a minor fire—your best bet would be to remove the damaged material as far as the first un-

How To Patch a Breakthrough in Gypsum Board

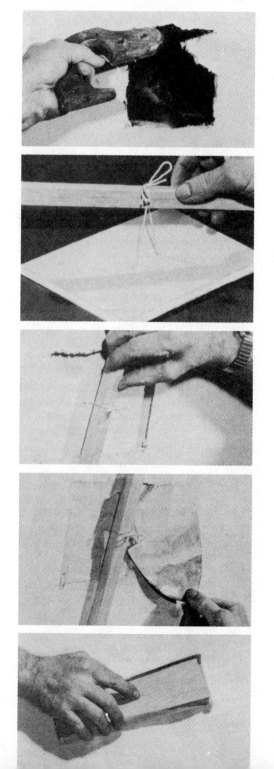

1. First cut the hole to a more or less rectangular shape, using a keyhole saw. Undercut two opposing sides, so that they bevel back under the board. Cut the other two sides so that they are beveled on the front. This trick keys the patch against movement into the wall or out.

2. Cut a piece of gypsum board about 2 inches bigger than the hole. Punch two nail holes through it, thread a piece of heavy cord through the holes, and loop it around a scrap of wood as shown here.

3. Insert the gypsum board through the hole, into the wall, and then snug it up tight against the back of the gypsum board by twisting the stick until the cord is tight.

4. Fill the depression with patching plaster, working around the stick and the string. Get as much plaster in place as possible. Then, let it harden. When it is hard, cut the string away and patch the rest of the area.

5. Sand off any high spots, and finish up with a final application of patch.

Using a Patch Kit

Start repair of hole caused by door knob by cutting out 4-inch square around damage, using special patch in kit as a template.

Insert special clips in edges of the hole. These hold the patch in place.

After patch has been inserted in clips, apply spackle to the area and smooth out evenly.

When surface is dry, sand the area until smooth; it is now ready to paint.

damaged joint. Then go at the job as though it were a new gypsum board project (see Chapter 4).

Extensive damage might also be the stimulus toward an entirely different wall. For instance, you might switch to paneling for the entire wall, rather than spend time and money putting it back into its original form.

7

Painting Interiors

No phase of home improvement and up-keep has fallen so completely into the hands of the home handyman as painting. The job is simple. The tools are simple. The results produced by an amateur can be equal to those bought from a professional. For many homeowners there is another factor; painting is fun, because the results are visible almost instantly.

A good, quick paint job depends on the selection of materials and colors, as discussed in the preceding chapter, plus the proper selection of tools and the proper step-by-step procedures.

The basic tools for painting are the brush and the roller. Some painters like to use spray equipment, and some of the modern sprayers are suitable for work indoors. But the clean-up problems caused by over-spraying and "drift" can sometimes out-weigh the advantages of speed–which is really not much greater than roller painting.

WHY A GOOD BRUSH IS IMPORTANT

Among the most seriously misguided do-it-yourself painters are those who think a cheap paintbrush can produce a good paint job. Never. Even in the hands of experi-enced professionals, a bad brush will leave its mark. Conversely, a good brush makes it possible for a rank beginner to lay on a smooth paint job, and do it quickly.

When you buy a paintbrush, insist on these characteristics:

● Avoid short bristles. The length should be about half again as great as the width of the brush. In other words, a brush that is $1\frac{1}{2}$ inches wide should have bristles about $2\frac{1}{4}$ inches long. If they are much shorter than this rule-of-thumb, they are likely to be too stiff. When you get into wider brushes—the kind called "wall brushes"—the rule changes, and you can get a good paint job out of a 4-inch brush with bristles only 4 inches long. (If you're buying a narrow brush, the rule changes in the other direction; a 1-inch brush should have bristles about 2 inches long—and the same is true even of a $\frac{1}{2}$-inch brush.)

The reason bristle length is important is the need for flexibility, not only to produce a smooth layer of paint, but to work into corners and crevices as is frequently neces-sary when you paint around trim.

● Look for tapered bristles. The best brushes were, originally, made of hog bristle, which tapered naturally. When natural bristles became scarce and expensive, better brush manufacturers started making nylon bristles deliberately shaped like the natural variety. Cheap brush makers took another path and started cutting natural bristles in two, to get two brushes for the price of enough bristles for one good brush. The square cut ends have a scraping action making it impossible to get a smooth finish. Still another bad product from the cheap manufacturers is a nylon bristle that is square cut–like strands of fine, fine wire. Again, smoothing is impossible.

● Examine the bristles carefully to see if the ends are "flagged." This means tips that are split into several fibers even smaller than the tapered end of the bristles. The flagged tip makes the smoothest application possible.

The research and effort that has been put into such nylon bristles as the type called Tynex has given us a synthetic bristle that equals or outperforms natural bristles in every way. And in one way, the nylon bristle completely eliminates the natural. Water thinner paints require nylon bristles, since the water softens natural bristles, making them too limp for good painting. Nylon, on the other hand, retains its springiness.

Some producers of synthetic bristles are coloring them black to make them look like natural bristles. Also, the natural black hog bristle is beginning to find its way back to the market. Most synthetic bristles are a honey-gold color, and, if purchased carefully, they will give you the best performance over the longest period of time.

● Although the bristle is the working element of a paintbrush, the handle and the ferrule are important, too. And, they are marks of quality and long life. The handle should be smooth and well shaped, so it fits comfortably into your hand. The ferrule—

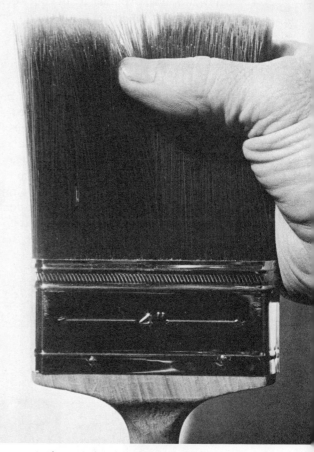

The secret of a good paintbrush is tapered and flagged bristles that are almost zero-thin at the tips. Examine brush as shown here. Avoid brushes with bristles that are square cut—the cheapest kind. Bristle length is important too.

the metal encasement that holds the bristles and the handle together—should be attached firmly to the handle.

A brush that meets the foregoing requirements will always give you a smoother, faster job. It may cost two or three times as much as one of the bargain-bin varieties. But, if you take care of a paintbrush (see below) it will last you the life of your house, and it will give you better results every time you use it.

How many brushes do you need? If you are working with paint and enamel only, you need three brushes. If you work with both paint and enamel *and* varnish, you need six. Why? Experts don't like to use brushes for both paint and varnish. There is a dangerous tendency for the pigments to linger in the brush and contaminate the clear finish.

Of course, if you do a lot of painting around the house, and if it is both a hobby and a money saver, you may want to go in for as many as nine different brushes. Some

of them are specialized. Some are routine.

● The wall brush is the paint spreader. For normal use, it should be 4 inches wide. You paint a little more slowly with one that is 3½ inches wide. Women often prefer the 3-inch width, because it is a little easier to handle.

● The trim brush is narrower—down to about 2 inches—and intended for painting woodwork, doors, and the like, which are a little more delicate.

● The sash tool is somewhat specialized. It is intended for use on windows, where cutting along the glass is difficult, and inevitably messy with a standard brush. The best tool for this job is the "angled"

Three brushes will do the majority of painting around the house. They are (top to bottom) a trim brush, a wall brush, and a sash tool—as it is called. The wall brush does a fast job in the 4-inch width, but can be 3 inches for somewhat easier handling. Distinguishing feature of the sash tool is the angled tip.

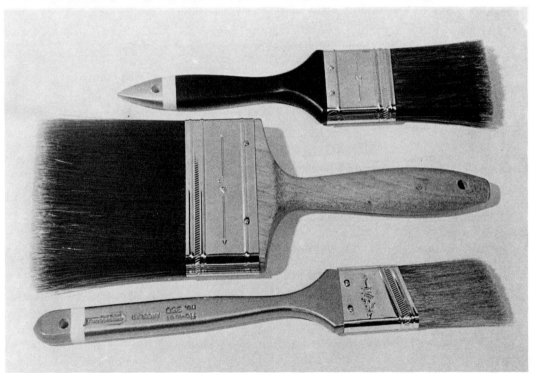

sash tool which has the ferrule at a slight angle, producing a business end that is at an angle. Used properly, this angled sash tool will give you well painted mullions and muntins, with little or no unwanted paint on the glass. The most useful width in sash tools is 1½-inch or 1-inch.

PICK THE RIGHT ROLLER

There's less to keep in mind in choosing a good roller than in choosing a good brush. However, remember to follow the same general rule: buy a good roller and take care of it. Cheap roller handles have a tendency to freeze and cause the roller to skid rather than roll. Cheap roller covers do not carry

much paint. They give you less coverage per load, and are therefore slow on the job. They tend to produce unwanted thick-and-thin patterns on the wall.

Roller handles. The roller cover slips on the handle of all but some specialty tools. One type has a metal cylinder over which the cover slides. Another is composed of several flexible metal rods arranged to fit inside the cover. You'll find this type useful because there is no tendency for the cover to get stuck on the handle, as sometimes happens with the metal cylinder type.

Handles come in two standard roller widths: 7 and 9 inches. Obviously, the 9-inch width will spread paint faster. It is not

Roller handle with "ribs" to hold the roller cover has less tendency to freeze the cover in place if paint dries inside.

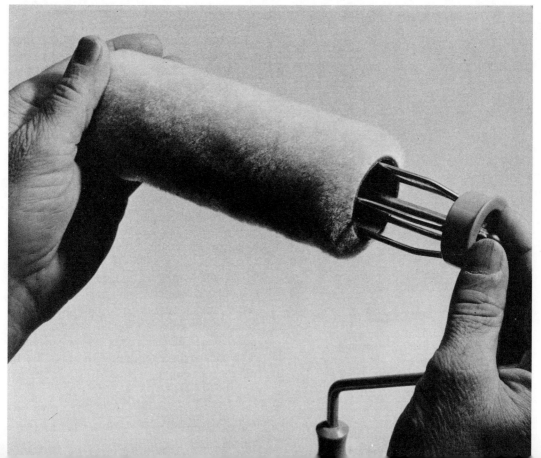

Paint stores sell roller handles that are a foot or so longer than ordinary handles. With them you can reach ceilings or the tops of walls without needing something to stand on.

as easy to use as the 7-incher, however, because if you twist it slightly it smears or skids over a larger area.

A further consideration in handle selection is the length of the actual handle. You can find standard rollers with handles a couple of feet long. A more significant feature, however, is provision at the end of a short handle for a screw-in extension. In most cases this is the standard size and thread to accept a standard push broom handle. With such a handle screwed in place, you can reach high places or low (even floors and ceilings) while working in a comfortable and convenient position.

The actual handle of roller handles may be wood or plastic. Plastic is better, since repeated washing eventually ruins a wooden handle.

There are also rollers narrower than the standard sizes—as narrow as 2 inches and 1 inch. Their purpose is to work narrow areas, such as the space between two close-set windows, or the space between a door and a corner. If you have situations like this in your home, the narrow widths will pay for themselves in time saved, since you won't have to switch over to a brush to handle narrow areas.

Roller covers. The roller cover has come a long way since the paint roller first appeared. The best today are made of a synthetic pile which spreads paint smoothly and washes easily between uses. The pile, which is something like a very fine version of carpeting, is applied over a cylinder that fits the roller handle. If you buy a good cover, the cylinder will be plastic or screening material that will withstand many washings. Cheap covers are made with cardboard tube core, and must be considered short-lived, finished after a few washings. The cheapest are too fragile to be washed at all without coming apart.

To avoid this messy problem, avoid rollers with nap that is too long and too flimsy to retain a certain stiffness when used in water-thinned paints. Synthetic fibers are best.

When you shop for a roller cover, let these features be your guide:

For typical wall work, the pile, or nap, should be about ¼ inch long. This length, in a good roller, will produce a perfectly smooth job. However, if a wall is rough, a longer nap may be necessary so that the roller will reach into the depressions.

The density of the pile—how close together the fibers are—is another consideration. If the cover is too dense, paint can't get in between the fibers, and the load is actually only on the tips. Spread a little farther apart, the fibers take up paint for their entire length, and a roller load covers a large area.

The thickness of the fibers is also important. If they are too small—limp, flimsy— they merely mat down and don't spread. On the other hand, fibers that are too stiff tend to spread the paint unevenly.

Add to these features the importance of

The range of roller covers is great. The two at the left are intended to produce textures, with their carpetlike pile. Next is a cover of sponge rubber. The remaining five represent the range of pile length.

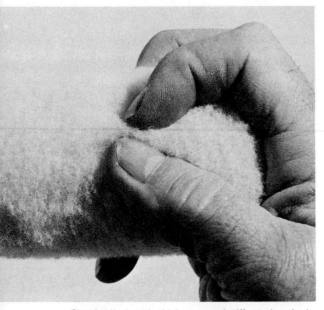

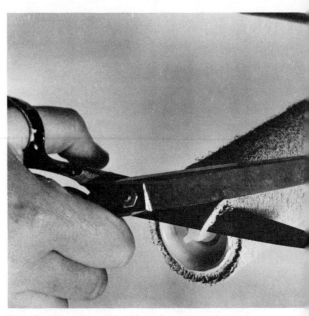

Check pile length, thickness, and stiffness by pinching it between your fingers. Pile shown is about half an inch long, tightly spaced, and springy.

If a roller is not beveled at the edges, use scissors to trim it into shape.

Range of shapes in rollers and roller covers: (A) standard 7-inch cover; (B) the 9-incher; (C) narrow roller for use in confined areas, such as between windows; (D) conical shape for working into corners; (E) a V-shaped roller excellent for working grooves in paneling; (F) inch-wide roller for extremely narrow strips of wall.

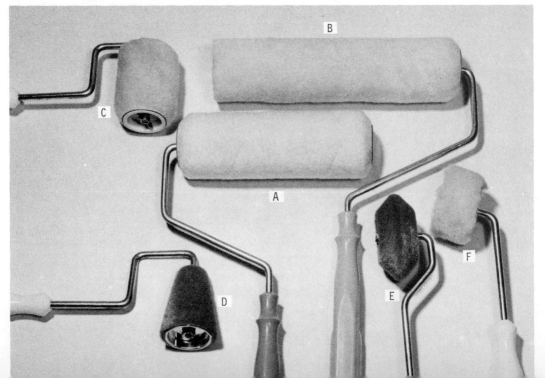

the shape of the cover. It must be a cylinder, of course, in order to roll smoothly. An important refinement, however, is a slight bevel at the ends of the cover, so that the edges of a roller stroke tend to blend into nothing. Without this bevel, the roller may leave tiny ridges of overthick paint that are difficult to roll away. If you have a roller that is not beveled, use scissors to cut it to the best shape (see photo).

Two special shapes that you may want in your roller collection are conical and V. Their purpose is to work in corners. You don't have to use a brush to "cut in" if you work with one of the special corner rollers.

The roller tray. In its standard form, the roller tray has a "tank" at one end that holds the paint. A ribbed area slopes up from the tank. You load the roller by dipping it in the paint, then make the load even by rolling it on the sloped area. Excess paint drains back into the tank while you are rolling the load on the wall.

In purchasing a tray, just keep in mind that one made of aluminum will live rust-free through many sessions with water-thinned paints and subsequent cleaning with hot water and detergent. Also, it makes sense to buy the size that will accommodate the 9-inch roller. Not only can you use the wider tool when you want to, but the wide tray holds more paint and speeds up the whole project when you use narrower rollers.

If you have a lot of painting to do, one additional piece of roller equipment worth looking into is the power-feed version. In simple terms, it involves a means of locking a standard gallon-size paint pail into a compressor circuit. The compressor (same as the one used for spraying) forces air into the can. The air forces the paint up a tube to the roller. It is by far the fastest method of

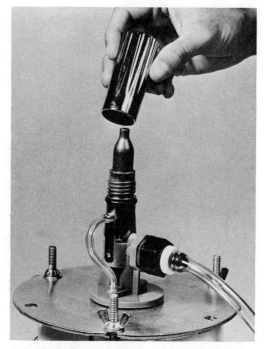

A simple device that feeds paint through a tube into a roller. It clamps over a gallon paint can; then a CO_2 cartridge provides the pressure.

applying paint to a wall, and if you control the feed carefully it can be one of the smoothest.

Special painting gadgets. Some paint applicators are not rollers and they are not brushes. The only word that fits them is "daubers." The dauber is a flat surface covered with a nap similar to roller nap, but with much shorter pile. You load it by dabbing it in a smear of paint (a roller tray works); then you draw it smoothly and slowly across the surface. A natural semi-vacuum created between the dauber and the surface transfers the paint to the wall. Daubers come in a variety of sizes, some with small handles, some engineered to accept screw-in handles.

Special paint "daubers" smear paint on the wall — and do it surprisingly smoothly. Typical forms are shown here.

STEP-BY-STEP PAINTING PROCEDURE

One of the most time-saving of all wall-painting procedures is getting rid of the interruptions all at once. Follow these steps:

● Move all the furniture to the middle of the room, leaving yourself room to work along all four walls. If the room is small, stack the furniture so as to make two adjacent walls available. Then restack it to provide access to the other two walls.

● If there is a loose rug on the floor, flip it back from the walls, so that it won't be paint-spattered. If the floor covering is permanent, spread newspapers or drop cloths. A good form of covering is cheap building paper, in rolls, or rolls of plastic.

● Take down all pictures and other hangings. Remove all switch and outlet plates. Paint them later if they are to match the wall. If there are wall fixtures, demount them and paint the small area immediately around them, feathering the edges. Then, when you go at the entire wall, you don't have the problem of cutting around the fixtures.

Whether you are using brush or roller to paint the walls of your room, there are certain procedures that generally save time and make the job easier.

● Trim should be painted first. Even if it is the same color — and even if it is the same paint — it is easiest to paint the trim, because any paint that slops off on the wall needs only to be feathered out so there is no dimension to the slop-over. It will disappear when you paint the wall, and it is much, much easier to cut the wall paint into the wall.

● Paint the smallest wall first. That is, one of the walls across the shorter dimension of the room—or a wall that may be mainly windows or doors or both. This gives you a chance to work into the job— into the materials, tools, and methods—on smaller areas, before you go at the bigger walls. Any mistakes—or changes of opinion as to color, etc., are quicker and easier to remedy on the smaller wall areas.

● Paint ceilings before you paint walls, by all means. (See the section later in this book on ceiling treatment.) If you paint the walls first, one of your biggest problems later on will be to keep paint from splattering on the walls when you paint the ceiling.

● If there is a picture molding along the wall at the ceiling, paint it the same color as the wall. Standard shapes in picture molding leave a little space between the top of the strip and the ceiling. It is easy, therefore, to paint along the molding without hitting the ceiling. On the other hand, if the wall is to be papered, the picture molding is usually painted the color of the ceiling.

You'll get a room painted most quickly and with the fewest problems if you follow these steps.

1. Start in a corner at the ceiling, standing on a safe ladder or a chair. Cut into the corner from the ceiling down to a level you can reach easily from the floor.

2. Paint across the top of the wall as far as you can reach easily without moving the ladder.

3. Fill in the triangle thus formed. Feather the edges into the unpainted area.

Work across a wall on a diagonal, as shown in these two photos. First paint along the ceiling, then downward at an angle. This way, any drips land on wall yet to be painted. Start with a W, as shown; then fill in the area, feathering the edge.

The same on-the-diagonal technique works with a brush. Drips on the wall are smoothed out when you work the next diagonal strip.

4. Move the ladder and paint a comfortable distance across the top of the wall, then a diagonal strip down to where it hits the corner.

5. Repeat this diagonal process across the wall. After two or three strips, you'll be hitting the baseboard at the bottom. Paint close to it, then cut carefully along the top edge.

When you come to a door, work across it completely, cutting close to it and the picture mold. Then cut down the near side to the baseboard. Cut down the opposite side using the same techniques as you did starting back.

Windows usually are surrounded by wall on all four sides. Cut across the top and down the near side, as with a door. Cut across the bottom of the window and along the baseboard. Then go back to the ceiling and cut down the far side, just as you did with doors.

Important: If you are right-handed, go around the room counterclockwise. If you work with your left hand, move clockwise. By doing this, you keep yourself opposite an unpainted area at all times, reducing the chances of smearing either the job or yourself.

PAINTING WITH A ROLLER

One of the nuisances of roller painting is switching back and forth between the roller and a brush (or specialist roller) to cut edges. Using latex paints, you can eliminate this nuisance by doing all the cutting first. Be sure to feather the edges out to zero, so there is no physical or dimensional layer of paint. If you do this, you can then complete the roller painting job without any lapmarks showing. It is important to realize, however, that this may be impossible with oil-base paints, since they lay on thicker and after the cutting has dried, lapmarks might show.

These tips will make you a roller expert right from the start.

1. Start right, by dampening the roller with water, or paint thinner if the paint is oil base. Roll out the excess on a scrap of lumber or on a spot of the wall that will not be painted for several hours) so it will have time to dry away. You can roll out excess water on newspapers, but not thinners, which might soften the ink and dirty the roller.

2. Load the roller carefully and fully at the beginning to make sure paint works in between the fibers. This will give you the

maximum amount of paint for each loading.

2. Lay on the load in a series of zigzag strokes, starting in an upper corner. Keep zigzagging until the roller has delivered all of its load. Then switch to smooth, even parallel strokes across the original deposit, to spread it evenly.

4. Finish the area with slow, light strokes that start in the unpainted area and roll into the paint. At the end of the stroke, raise the roller slowly, so that it leaves no mark. *Do not* lift the roller unless it is in slow motion either forward or backward.

5. Drop down to the next unpainted area. Repeat the zigzag operation, ending it just below the finished patch above.

6. Smooth the new application, and blend it into the previous patch.

Continue this operation until you reach the baseboard. Then start at the top again.

Two basic roller techniques are important. First, always start with an upward stroke, so that the paint doesn't puddle below the roller and run down the wall. Second, be careful not to run the roller so rapidly that centrifugal force causes it to spray droplets of paint all over everything.

PAINTING WITH A BRUSH

The techniques of painting with a brush are more exacting than with a roller, but a little practice makes you an expert in short order — especially if you follow the brush-buying tips presented earlier.

Start the job by dampening the bristles of the brush to condition them — to make them pick up more paint with each dip — and to make cleaning the brush easier at the end of the job. Remove excess liquid by gently striking the ferrule over the edge of your palm.

Start with the right can, too. Although nine out of ten painters work out of the can the paint came in, you might be that tenth painter who ladles the paint into a separate can, as needed. This keeps the rim of the can from gumming up with paint and, as a result, you can close the can factory-tight and avoid losing paint due to skinning over and other deterioration during storage time. Paint stores sell special plastic pails that hold perhaps a half gallon, excellent for this purpose.

Dipping tips. Never dip the brush more than about half the length of the bristles into the paint. If you do, the heel of the brush will gradually fill with paint and be next to impossible to clean.

With the first dip, move the brush around a bit in the paint, to open the bristles and let the brush fill completely. It helps pick up a full load if you sort of "jab" the brush gently into the paint with each dip.

Modern latex paints are thick enough so that generally you won't have to use the old technique of squeegeeing the excess paint off on the edge of the can, or slapping the brush against the inside of the can. Just lift the brush clear and let it drip for a couple of seconds. Then you can carry a full load to the wall.

Brushing techniques. After the first two or three loads, you will be able to estimate the amount of wall area each dip will cover. Lay the paint on the wall over that square footage without any concern about smoothness. All you are doing is getting the load on the wall. When this is done, go over the area with a gentle back-and-forth brushing technique, spreading the paint smoothly and uniformly.

Finish off the brushload with careful, one-direction strokes from the bare area into the painted area, and from the newest coverage into adjacent areas. Only the tips of the bristles should hit the wall during this final operation. When you are through, the

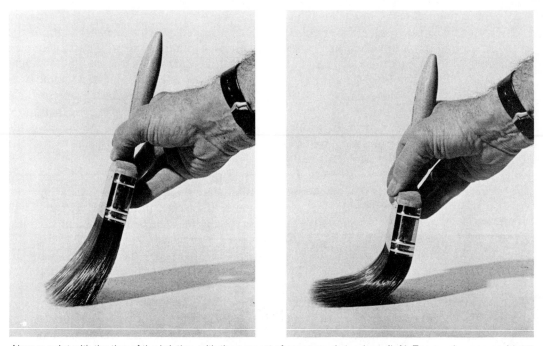

Always paint with the tips of the bristles, with the amount of pressure shown here (left). Too much pressure (right) tends to squeegee the paint off, rather than lay it on, and leaves a rough deposit.

area will be smooth and uniform and perfectly blended into the previously painted areas.

Painting trim. The principle requirement for trim painting is patience. Quite often, the trim in a room will take more time to paint than the walls and the ceiling.

Baseboards and picture molding are relatively simple. They involve nothing more than lengthwise strokes and careful cutting along edges. Windows and doors are tougher. Try these steps to make the job quicker and easier.

Windows. Start by removing the hardware, a less time-consuming job than cutting around them as you paint. If you have double-hung windows, lower the upper

sash and raise the lower sash as the first step. Paint the surfaces of the meeting rails that come together when the window is closed. Paint the top and bottom faces of the sash and meeting rails. Also, paint two or three inches along the mullions and the sash where they join the meeting rails.

Then close the windows until the meeting rails almost come together, but do not close the window tight until the paint has dried. Continue the painting with windows in the slightly open position, working from the edges of the paint on the mullions and sash.

It is easiest to paint windows from the inside out. Work first on the mullions. Let $1/8$ inch of paint lap over on the glass, to help form a seal against the weather. Do the sash—the frame—last.

It is standard practice to avoid overpaint-

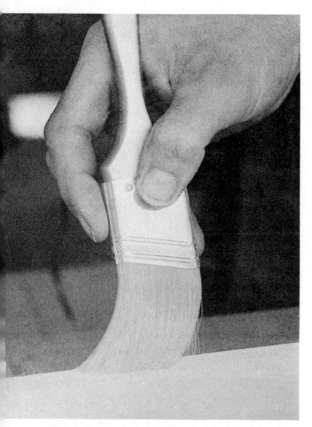

This is the way to hold the angled sash tool, brushing with the longer side leading. That way, the bending of the bristles provides a straight row of tips where they hit the sash.

The angle of the sash tool has its advantages, also, when you paint picture mold and in some other corner situations. Held as shown here, the handle is free from the adjacent area, but an even row of tips hits the surface being painted.

ing the channels the windows slide up and down in. Too much paint can make the windows stick. That is why the inside surfaces of window framing are rarely painted after the first time.

Doors. Here the techniques are similar. If the door is flush, paint it with brush or roller. If the door is paneled, start by painting the panels first, then the shaped edges of the frame around the panels. If you want to speed up the job, use a roller on the frame.

(Removal of the hardware on doors is more difficult than it is on windows, but with some simple hardware, you may prefer removal to cutting around.)

CARE OF BRUSHES AND ROLLERS

If you can take care of a paint job in one session, brush and roller care means nothing more than a thorough cleaning at the end of the operation. Hang the brush bristles down to dry. (Drill a hole through the

Paint doors from the inside out, the same as windows. After the panels are finished, the frame of the door can be painted with a roller.

handle if there isn't one.) Leave the roller cover on the handle and hang it to dry.

When a job takes two sessions with a layover between, it is not necessary to clean the brushes or roller used in latex paint if you use this trick: put the roller or brush in a plastic bag (such as a sandwich bag) that is big enough to cover it completely. Stand the plastic-bagged brush or roller in a can of water deep enough to come above the bristles or cover the roller. The pressure of the water against the outside of the bag forces it into contact with the bristles and the leftover paint. When you peel off the bag, the brush or roller is ready to continue with the job.

8

Get the Hang of Hanging Paper

Although paint is no doubt the easiest finish you can put on your walls, the most interesting is wallpaper or one of the flexible paper-like sheet-form materials. The selection of patterns is endless and the variations in application numerous. And paper can be combined with other wall materials to increase beauty and utility. The classic example in this category is the wall with a wainscot of paneling down where the wear and tear occur. Above is the wallpaper, up where the eye meets it more closely and can appreciate the greater visual interest, and where the wall is less likely to be subjected to physical damage.

Many homeowners who would gladly tackle any paint job around the house are reluctant to try papering. What about wrinkles? How do you keep things straight? Do the patterns always match? How much paper do you need? How do you cut the strips of paper to the right length? These are some of the questions, and the answers are all simple.

SELECTING A WALLPAPER PATTERN

Since wallpaper is an accent surfacing, unlike the monotone of paint, some important factors must be kept in mind: colors, and patterns; the rooms where wallpaper will be used; and which walls of those rooms should be papered.

Experienced and thoughtful interior decorators have some generalizations about wallpaper selection which you can consider along with your own ideas.

● If a room has many physical "breaks" in its walls, such as windows, doors, a fireplace, or a wall of shelves, it should be papered with a "quiet" paper. Small patterns in soft colors, stripes without much

A room decorated with such ornate accessories as this candelabra may call for a plain background, yet a gentle, intricate pattern such as this one from Abitibi produces an overall effect of good design.

contrast, or even "tone on tone" papers may be best. (In fact, paint may be a better —and easier—answer than paper.)

● Similarly, if a wall is used as a hanging place for many pictures or other decorations, it should provide a plain and simple background.

● Activity rooms are usually less "frantic" if they have relatively unfrenzied wall treatment. This counteracts the somewhat common opinion that the game room is the place for the wild wallpaper.

● Generally speaking, the rooms best suited for the strongest patterns are those where you spend relatively little time. A dining room, for example, might be pleasantly livable with a paper that rivals the bouquet on the table. The living room, in contrast, might be better with more reserved tones and patterns, aimed at maintaining peace and quiet over longer periods of time.

● Most important of all is the way the room is furnished. Some traditional furni-

A relatively simple paper pattern can provide the base for attractive decoration. These bird prints are being wallpaper-pasted over existing wallpaper.

ture settings demand wallpaper in keeping with this style. However, regardless of its style, if your furniture is strong in shape and design, you will be safe choosing relatively plain wallpaper. On the other hand, some smooth, straightline modern settings show off their simplicity best against strongly patterned backgrounds. Most well-managed wallpaper stores have literature or personnel that can help you with the selection of wallpaper designed for specific furniture styles.

● The size of the room has tremendous influence on the style of paper and also on the way it is used. As mentioned earlier in this book, bright strong colors make a room seem smaller. However, this does not make strong and bright wallpaper the logical candidate for large rooms. Too much pattern on large walls can mean just that: too much

pattern. This is why many homeowners like to use wallpaper on only one or two walls of big rooms and paint the others the color of the wallpaper background. The result is liveliness without frenzy.

A final consideration in the selection of a wallpaper is the condition of the walls. If they are smooth and even, any paper will work. But walls that are rough, perhaps inadequately patched, will reveal the shortcomings most graphically with a paper of fairly uniform tone. A strong pattern, or, even better, a textured material, will help hide the deficiencies.

HOW MUCH PAPER DO YOU NEED?

Two factors make it a bit difficult to determine the amount of paper you need for a room. In the first place, paper is priced "per

Wallpaper above paneling gives you the decorative effect of paper plus the utility of a painted wall below it, in the wear area. Here paneling is used at the head of a bed, which is exposed to wear and soil.

single roll" and most requirement figures are stated "per single roll." However, paper is always sold in double rolls or triple rolls. The second complication arises from the patterns themselves. Some are more "wasteful" than others because they require careful matching of the pattern, edge to edge (see below).

Despite all this, you can come close to actual requirements by this bit of arithmetic.

Measure the length of the room in feet — times two.

Measure the width of the room in feet — times two.

Add the two figures together.

Measure the height of the wall in feet.

Multiply the height of the wall by the total length of the walls in feet.

Divide this figure by 30. (A single roll contains 30 square feet.)

This will give you the number of single rolls your room will take, or half as many double rolls, or a third as many triple rolls, with a little to spare.

You might prefer to take the dimensions

and a general description of the room to the wallpaper dealer and let him work it out for you. He will surely (and wisely) recommend that you take an extra roll, to cover errors in calculations or accidents in hanging. Often, he will let you return unopened rolls, unless it is a special order.

Generally, it is unnecessary to try to figure how much square footage will be saved by doors and windows, except when you have a double-width doorway that may go clear to the ceiling. Very often the area represented by windows and doors will be needed to make up for unavoidable waste or the paper will hit a door or window in a way that requires full strips of paper, even though much of it may be cut out to provide the opening.

The following table will help you to determine the amount of paper you'll need. Keep in mind that needs are expressed in "single" rolls, but paper is sold only in double and sometimes triple rolls.

GETTING READY TO PAPER

Preparing a wall for paper involves the same procedures as those required for painting, but they do not have to be as meticulous. Paper covers up a good deal of superficial irregularity in a wall surface since it will bridge tiny cracks and crevices. Therefore, all you must do is fill wide gaps (which may require structural, not only surface repair) into which the paper might sink, showing the irregularity beneath it.

Judge a wall for papering on the basis of these considerations:

New walls. A wall that has no finish on it, whether it be gypsum board or plaster, should be *sized* before it is papered. Sizing is a sort of sealer mixed with water. You brush it on with a wide wall brush. It sinks

into the plaster or the paper facing of the gypsum board. When it dries, it leaves a surface to which regular wallpaper will stick tight. If you should ever decide to remove the wallpaper, the sized wall will release it much more readily than a wall over which paper has been applied without sizing.

Painted walls. You can apply wallpaper over any wall which is painted with a *nonglossy* finish. The wallpaper paste will stick very well to flat paint, and almost as well to semiglossy paint. But a glossy paint must be treated, or adhesion may be inadequate. Either swab the wall with a strong solution of trisodium phosphate, to cut away the gloss, or coat it with sizing before you paper. There are special materials for this type of sizing. Consult with your paint and paper dealer for the type that will work best in your situation.

Dirty walls. Ordinary soiling, such as you might find in living rooms or bedrooms, presents no problem. However, if the wall is in an area of the house that is subject to oily dirt, it should be washed with trisodium phosphate.

PLANNING THE PAPERING

Any paperhanger worth the name looks upon a graphically designed paper as a picture that must be centered on the area. If the wall happens to be an exact complement of the widths of the roll, there is no problem. Start in one corner and end in the other. However, this rarely happens.

You must, therefore, do your planning as though you were going to start hanging paper in the center of the wall and work both ways. Which, incidentally, is the best way to do it. The question becomes: Do

CEILING HEIGHT	8 Feet	9 Feet	10 Feet	11 Feet	12 Feet	
Size of Room	Single Rolls	Single Rolls	Single Rolls	Single Rolls	Single Rolls	Yards of Border
8x10	9	10	11	12	13	13
10x10	10	11	13	14	15	15
10x12	11	12	14	15	16	16
10x14	12	14	15	16	18	17
12x12	12	14	15	16	18	17
12x14	13	15	16	18	19	18
12x16	14	16	17	19	21	20
12x18	15	17	19	20	22	21
12x20	16	18	20	22	24	23
14x14	14	16	17	19	21	20
14x16	15	17	19	20	22	21
14x18	16	18	20	22	24	23
14x20	17	19	21	23	25	24
14x22	18	20	22	24	27	25
16x16	16	18	20	22	24	23
16x18	17	19	21	23	25	24
16x20	18	20	22	24	27	25
16x22	19	21	23	26	28	27
16x24	20	22	25	27	30	28
18x18	18	20	22	24	27	25
18x20	19	21	23	26	28	27
18x22	20	22	25	27	30	28
18x24	21	23	26	28	31	29

you put a *seam* in the center of the wall, or do you put a strip of paper in the center?

Start by measuring to find the middle of the wall. Then, with a roll of paper or a strip of wood as long as the paper is wide, start at the middle and work to a corner, marking the width of the roll successively across the wall. When you reach the corner, if you end up with *more than half of a roll*, the paper should be hung with a seam in the middle of the wall. If you end up with less than half a roll in the corner, you should start with a strip centered on the middle line of the wall. That way, you have the widest possible less-than-full strip at each corner, and the wallpaper picture will be centered on the wall.

Relatively simple, plain, soft paper does not need all this attention to balance on the

wall. A little thought will reveal that this centering method may leave mismatched pattern situations in the corners of the room. This should be of little concern; most wallpapered rooms have these mismatches and they are rarely noticed.

There are situations in which the positioning of windows and doors on a wall will make the "picture balance" either impractical or too difficult to warrant the effort. However, such situations are, in themselves, sufficiently unsymmetrical to overpower the relatively subtle lack of symmetry in wallpaper pattern positioning.

PREPARATORY WALLPAPERING STEPS

The first thing you need, if you are going to do your own papering, is a table on

Use the roll of paper itself as a gauge for determining whether a seam or a center goes in the middle of the wall. See text for specific techniques.

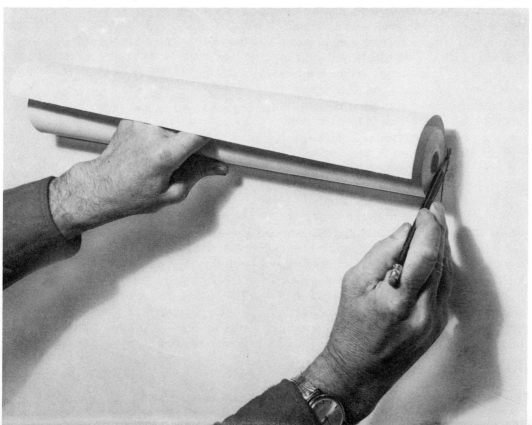

which to work. In the typical home with 8-foot ceilings, this means a sheet of plywood ripped lengthwise, giving you a work surface measuring 2x8 feet. Actually, a little longer would be handier, but most amateur paperhangers learn to work with 8 feet, because that's standard plywood length. If your walls are higher than 8 feet, you can make a table by cleating together three lengths of 1x10. If you are working with the 30-inch paper, make that three lengths of 1x12.

Lay this work surface across a pair of sawhorses, across the dining room table, or the backs of two sturdy chairs.

Unroll the first roll of paper, and study the pattern for a moment to see how the pattern itself may influence the hanging procedures. Virtually every wallpaper except simple stripes is an over-and-over repeat of a design. On the wall, these designs form an overall pattern—up and down and horizontally. With some designs it is offensive to the eye if the design unit is cut in two, although most designs can be cut exactly in half without becoming an eyesore.

When you hang such papers, you want an entire pattern shape at the ceiling level. It would be nice to have a complete repeat at the baseboard, too, but this is not critical since the baseboard area is less conspicuous and often hidden behind furnishings.

What all this means is that the roll of paper must be cut into lengths which have the proper pattern situation at the top—regardless of the length of the strip.

In practice, you cut, true and square, the end of the roll at the proper place to conserve the pattern. Then you unroll enough paper to run from the ceiling (or the picture molding) to *the top of the first complete pattern that falls below the required length* and cut it off. Repeat this until the roll is all cut into lengths, lying in a pile on the work table.

The repeat of a pattern is demonstrated here. Note that the part of the design at the lefthand edge coincides with the design on the righthand side—half a pattern-unit down. This means that the paper must be dropped or raised half a pattern with each succeeding strip. It also means that, at the ceiling, full patterns and half-patterns alternate.

There is another important consideration in accommodating the pattern. Many papers have a pattern repeat, vertically, that makes it necessary to match the edges properly. If you fail to do this, it may appear that the paper was hung at a slant, with rows of pattern running up or down hill. Thus, when you are cutting the rolls into proper lengths, check to make sure that the edge-to-edge fit of the patterns will be proper. In many cases you will find that this

Paste brush, wall brush, roller, and cutter are specialist wallpapering tools, along with a utility knife, cord for plumb bobbing, and a pail for paste.

matching will be automatic if you hang the strips you cut from the paper alternately, instead of the way they came off the rolls consecutively.

It is the practice of many experienced paperhangers to cut the top end of the strips carefully and cleanly, so they can be positioned properly at the ceiling. Then the excess falls at the bottom, where it is simple to cut it off in place.

The tools of paperhanging come into use in this order:

A yardstick or steel tape.

A pair of scissors. Regular paper hanger's shears are heavy and tough, but you can usually do the job with a good pair of ordinary household scissors. They are used for any true and smooth cutting required before the paper is on the wall.

A paste brush. This is a wide, fiber-bristled brush used to apply paste.

A wall brush, used to smooth the paper out and bring it into contact with the wall. There is no true substitute, although a long-nap paint roller has been used for the job.

The edge roller is a small wooden roller

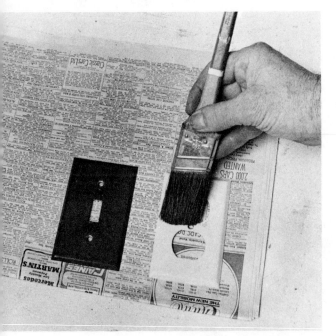

Remove all switch and outlet plates. Paint them the background color of the paper—or one of the pattern colors. Or cover them with actual wallpaper to coincide with the overall pattern. Many wall fixtures can be lowered to make papering around them easier.

length. Arrange the strips alternately, if that is part of the matching process. Then turn the pile over, with the nonpatterned surface up.

2. Slide the pile on the table so the tops of the strips are flush with one end, and one edge of the pile is flush with the edge of the table on the opposite side from where you will be standing. The paper will hang over the other end of the table (unless you have improvised a table of extra length), but this will be taken care of in following steps.

3. Slip the top sheet toward you, just to the edge of the table.

4. Spread paste (mixed according to instructions on the package or can it came in) over about two-thirds of the strip. Make sure that you cover the top edge and both side edges. The spread of paste should be about equal to a thick coat of paint.

5. Lift the top end of the strip and fold it over the pasted area, leaving a few inches of pasted paper exposed.

6. Slide the strip up—in the direction of the folded end—bringing the overhang, if any, up on the flat.

7. Continue spreading paste over the remainder of the strip, then fold it up the same way as you folded the top down, so that the two ends meet, but do not overlap.

The strip is now ready to hang, except that it must "season" for a few minutes. Fold the twice-folded strip in half and hang it over the back of a chair or lay it on a nearby surface, and do the pasting routine on the second strip. While you are doing this, the paste softens the paper of the first strip and makes it ready to go on the wall.

Now follow these instructions:

1. Apply paste to the second strip, fold it and put it aside to season.

2. Hang the first strip on the wall as explained below.

3. Brush paste on the third strip.

in a handle, used to press the edges of the paper tight against the wall.

Cutters are sharp or serrate-edged disks mounted in a handle so the edge can be rolled along the cut-off line. They are used for cutting after the paste has been applied to the paper.

Wallpaper tools, by and large, are almost in the gadget range, and cost very little. Buy them at a wallpaper or hardware store.

STEP-BY-STEP WALLPAPERING

1. When the foregoing matching and length problems have been worked out, cut two or three rolls of paper to the proper

Brush the adhesive over a little more than half the strip, making sure that you leave no voids.

Fold the pasted area over itself. Paste the other half and fold it—then let it "season".

4. Hang the second strip.

5. Paste the fourth strip . . . and continue.

This routine usually provides the right amount of seasoning time for each strip, and keeps the process going smoothly. It may be necessary to interrupt the routine from time to time, when you come to windows or doors or other obstructions that require so much time that the paste might dry or harden. When you meet such problems, apply paste and fold the strip; then *wait* until it has softened properly for hanging.

Putting the paper on the wall. The actual application of paper to the wall requires care, but no difficult techniques, once you get started. The first step is to establish a true vertical at the middle of the wall. Use a plumb bob and chalkline if you have one, or simply hang a fairly heavy object on one end of the string. A pair of scissors, a hairbrush, a Boy Scout knife—anything to act as a "bob." Position the other end of the string at the ceiling where the edge of the first strip will go. Remember, this will be either the exact center of the wall or exactly half a roll's width to one side of exact center, depending on the results of the operation previously explained. Snap the chalkline, or make careful pencil marks a foot or so apart along the hanging string. This establishes the line for the first strip of paper. All other strips will be vertical if you join them properly at the edges. Follow these steps:

1. Unfold the top half of the strip that has been seasoning. You will find that not only has the stiffness of the paper more or less disappeared, but the face-to-face position has helped distribute the paste uniformly.

2. Holding the paper by the edges, about 3 inches from the top, carefully position it so that the top edge is exactly at the ceiling,

To apply the sheet to the wall, unfold the top half. Carefully position the top edge of the sheet against the picture mold or the ceiling. Smooth it against the wall with the wide wallpaper brush.

or the picture molding if there is one. The edge of the paper should go precisely at the vertical line made with the plumb bob. You'll be standing on a ladder or a sturdy chair.

3. Maneuver the paper into contact with the wall. To do this you may nudge it with the heels of your hands, with your forearms —even with your forehead. When a fair amount of the strip has come into contact with the wall, you can let go of it. It may slide down the wall a little, but you can push it back up by placing your hands flat

To make the paper smooth, use the wallpaper brush in strokes from the center of the strip toward the edges. A good brush has just enough stiffness in the bristles so that they apply the proper pressure when they are about half bent. Be careful not to gouge the paper with the corners of the brush handle.

paper again, making sure that contact is complete.

Finally, go over the entire strip once more with the brush, using enough pressure to bend the bristles, forcing the paper against the wall.

At the bottom, you will have some overlap. Brush down into the corner formed by the top of the baseboard. Then tap the paper into that corner with the ends of the bristles. Pick up your cutter and run it along the wall across the top edge of the baseboard. The blade may not cut the waste off completely, but it will score or serrate the edge so that the waste will tear off easily.

Clean any wallpaper paste off the baseboard with a damp rag.

The final step is to run the roller along the edges and across the top and bottom. Do not use too much pressure or you may squeeze the paste out from beneath the paper. The purpose of the roller operation

against the surface and exerting upward pressure.

4. Using the wallpaper brush, start smoothing the paper into contact.

5. Check the vertical, to be sure the paper is straight up and down.

6. When the unfolded upper half of the paper is entirely in contact, reach behind the lower half and "peel" it downward.

7. Continue brushing the paper into contact, working from the top toward the bottom, until it is all in place.

At this point, check to see if there are any bubbles. This is easiest to do if you have a relatively strong light (such as a photoflood) that you can shine across the wall at a flat angle. If you find bubbles, slip a finger under the paper and lift it free of the wall in the area of the bubble. Then, holding the edge free, work the wall brush over the

If the paper doesn't smooth out against the wall, gently peel it away with one hand; then while holding the edge free, brush across the wrinkles or bubbles.

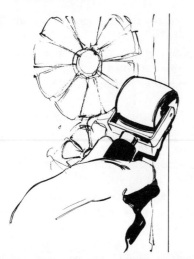

The purpose of the roller is to press the paper flat and tight at the edges, so that joints will not show. Do not, however, apply too much pressure or you may force the adhesive out from beneath the paper.

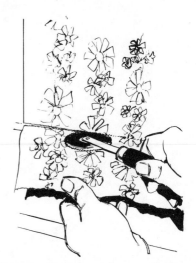

Run the cutter along the wall across the top edge of the baseboard, scoring the paper so that you can tear off the waste evenly.

is to make sure the edges are snug against the wall, tightly adhering, and flat.

Follow the procedures covered above with succeeding strips, working first to the right, then to the left, so that you alternate the joints. Be careful to match patterns carefully between the strips. Check constantly to make sure that the edges of the paper are butting neatly and completely together. Wipe off any paste that smears on the face of the paper, using a damp rag. Continue until you have finished the last two full-width strips, one on each side.

When you reach the corners, it will be necessary to cut a strip to fit, unless some rare coincidence should make the full width proper. This strip should be wide enough to cover the remainder of the wall *plus half an inch*. When you hang the strip, use the wallpaper brush to tap it into and around the corner. When you hang the paper on the adjacent wall, the final strip will not have the half inch of wrap-around; it will be cut

the exact width to reach into the corner, and will lap over that half-inch on the original wall.

Working around obstructions. When, in your lateral progression across the wall, you come to a door or window or other obstruction, your procedures will be determined by the amount of the next strip that will have to be removed to work around it.

● If only a few inches of the strip will reach into the obstruction, you can paste it as usual, and go through the hanging techniques covered above. The paper will, of course, lap the opening. Using scissors, make a diagonal cut from the edge into the corner or corners of the opening. Tap the paper in place with the wide brush, then use the cutter to remove the waste, the same as you did at the baseboard during run-of-the-wall hanging (see above).

● If half or more of the strip reaches into the space, it is simplest to rough-cut the strip before you brush paste on it. Make sure that the cutout is about an inch smaller on all sides than the actual opening. Then, apply paste to the piece and put it in place. Cut or tear diagonals at the corners. If there is a molding around the opening, let the paper lap up on that molding. When the strip is smooth, use the cutter in the corner, as you did at the baseboard (see above).

Across the top of doors and windows and across the bottom of windows, you'll need one or more short lengths, which must be cut to match the pattern. It is best to cut these short pieces from another roll, rather than to disrupt the continuity of strips already cut.

On the other side of the door or window, you will encounter again the need to cut out waste to finish across the top and bottom and down the side. Cut the shape roughly from a dry strip, apply paste, let it cure a few minutes, then use the same methods that worked on the other side of the window or door.

A final step, not necessary but a great convenience later on, is the application of a special coating that makes the wallpaper easier to keep clean. Roll it on, after the wallpaper paste is thoroughly dry.

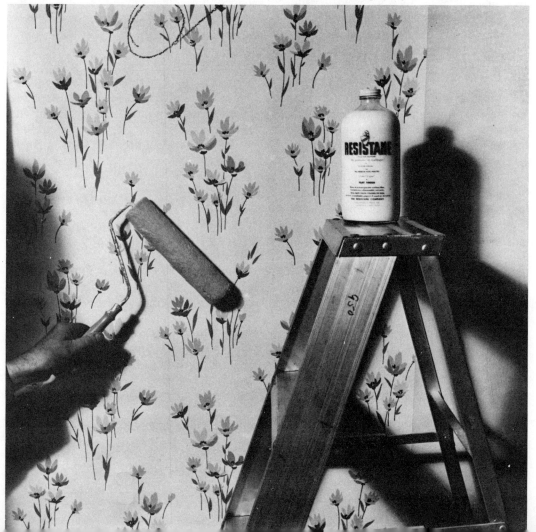

Prepasted papers. Some papers are manufactured with an adhesive on the back, applied at the factory. To use them, you dip the cut-to-length strips in water. The water softens the paper and liquifies the adhesive. All you have to do is put it in place, using the same techniques as those discussed on previous pages for regular paper.

There are some disadvantages, however. Many amateur paperhangers find that the soaking process is difficult. Actually, it is best done in the bathtub—an obvious nuisance. You can buy special wax-lined troughs to soak the paper in—but the slop-over is a nuisance. Most critical of all, the prepasted papers are truly adhesive only over an ideal base, such as sized gypsum board or plaster or flat latex-painted walls. And they do not have the slipperiness that lets you adjust the final position of the paper as easily as you can do it with regular paste.

For that reason, many paperhangers who find the exact pattern they want only in a prepasted paper handle it just as they would regular paper—brushing paste on it in the same way.

Untrimmed papers. All of the discussion thus far in the chapter has involved pre-trimmed papers. Such rolls are by far the most common, these days. However, you may find a paper you like in the untrimmed version.

A long time ago, both edges of the roll had a half-inch or so of margin. In those days, it was standard practice to trim the margin off one edge, and to lap that trimmed edge over the margin of the other edge. The idea of butted joints came along, but it did not completely replace the half-lap joint. Some paperhangers still prefer it; they are not to be considered old-fashioned for their preference. The lapped joint may reveal a little of itself because of the double thickness of paper. But, it never reveals itself because of gaps between the edges, as do butted joints.

To go back into the untrimmed days: After you apply paste to the paper, and fold it down over itself, then paste the other half and fold it *up* over itself, you lay a straight-edge over the paper, and with a razor-edged knife cut off the margin on one edge. This must always be the edge that will lie over the preceding *untrimmed* edge.

On the wall, make your adjustments of the strip so that the cut edge makes a match with the preceding untrimmed edge.

Many paperhangers complain about this lapped joint, but it is not obnoxiously visible if you roll it as flat as possible with an edge roller.

Borders. Time was when all wallpaper had borders pasted horizontally along the top of the wall, below the ceiling or picture mold. It may be that you'll pick a pattern and border combination. If you do, you can forget about making the edge at the top neat and clean. The border will cover it.

NONCONFORMIST PAPERING METHODS

Does paper always have to be hung in the traditional manner? No, and you may want to come up with some ideas of your own. Some very interesting walls have been done in modern settings with paper pasted at a 45-degree angle, forming a chevron effect. There may be no reason why a wallpaper pattern can't be used horizontally instead of vertically. Patterned papers may be used on ceilings, instead of the white paper that once was standard, or the white paint that is now used.

Your dealer may carry wallpaper squares —one of the more recent ideas in paper.

The squares go up one at a time, without the troubles of strips. People who have used them warn against allowing too much "seasoning" time after the paste goes on, or the result may be shrinkage on the wall that leaves gaps between squares.

In addition, there is no reason why wallpaper must be restricted purely to walls. It has been used often and effectively to decorate panels in doors or other flat areas normally considered suitable only for paint.

There are even attractive and distinctive settings in which homeowners have taken the time to cut out the graphic part of a wallpaper pattern and cement it to a background of water-base paint.

SPECIALTY WALLPAPERS

Although standard, but improved, wallpaper continues to be the most used of all, there are variations that have their place in today's overall wall-treatment scheme. Here are some of them:

Vinyl paper. A wallpaper with a coating of vinyl that makes it almost plastic in nature. Washability is excellent. There are problems with hanging, since the vinyl layer prevents the sheet from becoming as soft and flexible as ordinary paper.

Washable paper. This has a clear plastic surfacing which makes it almost as scrubable as paint. The surfacing is somewhat in the nature of waterproofing. It cannot be subjected to strong, heavy washing materials, but it will withstand the normal cleaning about as well as a painted surface.

Self-stick paper. This is coated with a material which is adhesive upon pressure. It can be applied like other self-stick materials and can be removed in the same way. A challenge, however, is the deterioration over a period of time of the release factor.

Some self-stickables come loose easily not long after they are applied, but the adhesiveness becomes irreversible after a period of aging. For that reason, a paper that is labeled strippable may be intended for use in temporary situations.

Texture finish papers. Standard wallpaper has always been made by printing patterns and colors on paper. The surface is smooth. The inks do not add to the thickness of the paper. The artistry of the printing may seem to present a dimension, but there is no true texture. Some wallpaper dealers now handle papers with a true texture. Some have the shape molded in the backing, others may have a coating of some nonpaper, nonink material. Common coatings are sand and flocking. Such papers go on the wall with the same procedures as ordinary paper, but with considerably more difficulty.

Murals. Many interesting and decorative murals are available in wallpaper form. Pick a large, unbroken wall and center a mural on it for a good variation in wall treatment. The murals come in several pieces, pasted up as though they were square-cornered parts of a jigsaw puzzle.

NONPAPER WALL COVERINGS

In many of the best stocked wallpaper stores, and in many of the burgeoning "home centers" and "panel centers," you'll find a variety of flexible, sheetlike wall coverings that are not paper. They cost considerably more than paper, but their distinctiveness — and in some cases durability — make them worth the extra price.

Hanging these materials is essentially the same as hanging regular paper, except that different adhesives and cutting techniques may be required. Your best bet is to confer with your dealer about hanging methods that work best with the specific material. Here are some of the more popular nonpaper wall coverings:

Fabric. This can range from denim to burlap to grass cloth to silk in natural or dyed colors.

Felt. This material, in wall-covering form, is laminated to a paper backing, so that it doesn't shrink or swell—and so the paste doesn't bleed through. It comes in many colors and gives an interesting look. It is also sound-deadening to a degree.

Cork. The sound-deadening feature of felt is also part of the advantage of cork, which comes in sheets of paper—thin cork laminated to a paper backing.

Wood. Advances in the techniques of slicing wood for plywood fabrication have led to slices so thin that they can be laminated to a plastic or paper backing and handled like paper.

A major advantage of wall coverings such as those listed above is the way they will cover walls that are not smooth and plane enough for regular wallpaper. They can even go over concrete block unless the mason was too hit-or-miss with his work.

9

A Review of Paneling

In one or another of the several physical forms of paneling, there are hundreds of designs and patterns. Some of them are wood and as traditional as great-grandfather's barnboards. Others are plastic and as modern as tomorrow's wildest decorator's dream. They all have great advantages over any other form of wall treatment; they go up fast, they last long, and their maintenance ranges from simple to zero.

Your selection of a paneling material will be based on these considerations:

● *The esthetic effect.* You can match the mood of any interior with paneling. You can use it for one wall or more in a room, along with other wall treatments, to achieve endless variety in background for living.

● *The physical requirements.* Some paneling materials are not only decorative, but an important part of the house structure.

● *Ease of handling.* Some paneling materials are cumbersome and heavy—and earn their way into the home because of exceptional beauty. Others earn their way because they are light and easy to handle—with no sacrifice in beauty.

● *Cost.* You can spend $100 or more for a sheet of exotic "architectural grade" wood paneling. You can pick up the same size sheet in a wood imitation hard to tell from the genuine thing at less than $5.

KINDS OF PANELING MATERIALS

Paneling comes in several forms, each with special advantages as a do-it-yourself item.

Plywood. This is one of the most common of all paneling forms. It is usually $1/4$-inch thick for home use (although there are $3/4$-inch panels aimed at the commercial market). Composition is normally three-ply. The face is a select sheet of the chosen wood. The back may be cast-off slices of the same wood or some entirely different species. The cross banding can be anything.

Plywood is also used as the backing for a face of plastic sheet, sometimes with an entirely realistic photographic reproduction of a rare wood or other material. The plastic is cemented to the three-ply backup.

Rough-cut cedar in plywood form gives the appearance of solid wood paneling at much lower cost. Many other true woods are put in sheet form in the same manner as this example from Evans.

Hardboard. No doubt the greatest variety in paneling "patterns" comes in the hardboard variety. The backing is the material familiarly known by the trade name Masonite, or Marlite. The hardboard sheet can be smooth or textured. It can look like the finest walnut. It can look like bricks. It can look like marble. In some finishes it is completely waterproof with a backing of "tempered" hardboard. It is also made in "filigree" patterns with perforations of various shapes that transmit light and permit one to see through. Another form, called "pegboard," has small holes spaced an inch apart, which accept hangers in a wide variety of forms (see Chapter 12).

Beautiful masonry wall, bricks below, stucco above? No. Textured hardboard in both cases, with antique-stained pine boards covering the joints in the Masonite paneling.

Particle board. This material, made from wood chips, can be used as a paneling material to be finished after installation. It is also the "core" for sheets faced with select wood species or other surfacing materials.

Asbestos board. This material is made of asbestos fibers bonded into sheet form with portland cement. It is fireproof, and proof against almost any other type of chemical or physical damage. In its natural form it is concrete gray, but it is also available prefinished.

Plastics. Some forms of paneling might not exactly deserve the name — although they do the job of paneling and are handled in much the same way. Through a sheet-forming process, plastic is molded into such textures as flagstone, slate, bricks, and other materials. It goes on the wall with adhesives, usually in units small enough to be easy for any member of the family to handle.

Wood. Last but not least is paneling made of solid wood. Redwood and pine (usually

Textured panels also come in patterns that are not imitations of wood or other building materials, such as this carved leaf design from Marlite.

Redwood paneling is available in tongue-and-groove stock 6 inches wide and as long as 24 feet.

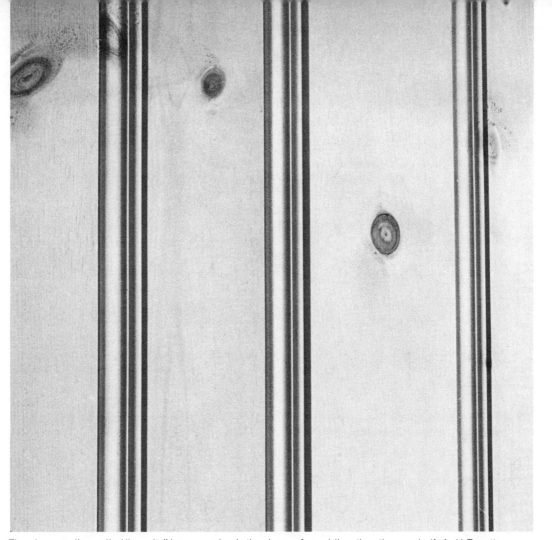

The pine paneling called "novelty" has one edge in the shape of a molding, the other one half of a V. Together, they form patterns like the one shown here, and the joint is completely concealed. Several other shapes are available.

knotty) are the most commonly used woods, but some dealers carry boards suitable for paneling in other species. The boards used for paneling are nominal-inch —actually very close to $3/4$-inch. The edges are tongue-and-groove and may also have some sort of a shape that helps conceal the joint. V-board is used a great deal; it is nothing more than bevels at the edges that come together and form a V. "Novelty" paneling has a bevel on one edge and a molding shape at the other. The two shapes combine at the joint to produce an interesting effect that makes the actual joint inconspicuous. Wood paneling is most often 8 inches wide—nominal. Because of millwork and the tongue-and-grooving, the actual face is 7 inches. Pine is available in all standard nominal widths from 4 inches up for "random width" paneling. In all widths, the face is about an inch less than the stated width.

Paneling doesn't always have to follow traditional lines. This redwood, installed in a diagonal pattern, makes an attractive stair wall.

Panels you make yourself. One of the most traditional of all paneling is called "raised." It is not commonly available commercially, but it is simple to make in a workshop equipped with a power saw. It is formed of a series of crossmembers and verticals which act as frames around single panels. Each panel is made of a length of 1x12 with the edges and ends beveled. The bevels fit into rabbets cut into the back side of the verticals and crossmembers. Details of the construction are given later in the pages on working with solid paneling.

Sizes and shapes. The most common forms of paneling are 4x8 sheets and 8 foot by 16-inch strips. The design and texture are usually handled in a way that allows nailing into standard 16-inch-on-center wall studs, with the nail heads disappearing into the pattern or texture. You can also get sheets longer than 8 feet — and shorter — when the ceiling height calls for the different dimensions. The cost is much greater, however, and many homeowners prefer to use some form of wainscot or "dropped ceiling."

The standard 16-inch by 8-foot strips are

Hardboard paneling is used in this room to create a striking dual surface. The wall at left is covered with Masonite paneling in a parquet-like design while the right-hand wall is given a rough, plaster look with Stuccato panel siding.

obviously planned for fastening to standard wall-stud spacing. In addition, they have a tongue on one edge and a groove on the other, so that the strips interlock as they go up.

Another form of paneling is sheets that are usually 16x16 inches. They have tongue-and-groove edges and interlock as they go up. Nailing is possible, but adhesives are usually better if the subwall is suited to adhesive application. The designs usually fall in with the square format and the look on the wall is much like decorative tile.

WHICH PANELING MATERIAL IS BEST?

The number of different paneling materials makes it possible to satisfy just about every requirement in residential wall treatment, and that makes it difficult to suggest which is best. First of all, it must meet your needs from the standpoint of appearance. Considering the fantastic range of woods, patterns, textures, and simulations that come in panel form, you should have no problem finding something to your taste.

Structurally, plywood in its heaviest forms is strongest. Thus, if you are paneling

Paneling in strip form is easier to handle than full 4x8 sheets, and often goes in place with invisible metal clips that simplify nailing. The joint is made a part of the overall design.

a new wall, you might first look at plywood sheets, which would supply both strength and beauty. However, a very close rival, structurally, would be hardboard.

In a damp situation, such as a basement wall, hardboard would be the best choice — and it is available in enough variations to meet decorative requirements.

In a *wet* situation, tempered hardboard materials such as Marlite are extremely serviceable — even serving as linings for shower stalls.

Any situation which presents an acknowledged chance of fire damage would surely call for the asbestos cement.

Another factor is your own distinct and irreversible preferences. If you are a true lover of wood, you probably won't be able to make yourself like any of the wood imitations even though it takes a mighty close look to tell the real thing from the fake, and the imitation might be entirely maintenance-free forever. The same can be said, of course, of imitation brick, slate, fabric, and other materials. If imitation of any kind bothers you, you may be unhappy with fakery that is, in many practical aspects, better than what it imitates.

Cost is another variable that runs full scale, and that influences decisions tremen-

Synthetic materials often combine well with natural—or traditional—materials. Actual wooden beams scavenged from an old barn are used here with a wormy-chestnut-like paneling from Marlite.

dously. Most of the paneling materials that are imitations exist because the real thing costs too much. Not every homeowner could afford to panel a den with rosewood, but almost any homeowner could afford that remarkable photo-process reproduction of rosewood on a hardboard backing.

Then there is architectural and decorative appropriateness. This makes itself felt most vitally in traditional settings. The house that is—or purports to be—a renovated mid-nineteenth-century barn really needs the old barn siding as paneling for the family room. True, there are some excellent barn sidings in hardboard simulations. But to those for whom authenticity is important the imitation can never be the solution.

TIPS ON BUYING PANELING

One problem you frequently encounter when you shop for real wood paneling is true match, sheet to sheet, in color and grain pattern. The extremely expensive architectural grade sheets bypass the problem by using veneers cut consecutively from the same log and maintained in units throughout the manufacturing process. This type of accuracy is likely to be more accidental than deliberate in the kind of quarter-inch plywood material that is within typical homeowner budgets.

The best way to go shopping for paneling:

● Find an outlet that has sheets *in stock*. When you order from small samples you may get what you thought you were going to get—but you may not.

● Determine in advance how many sheets of paneling you are going to need.

● Go through the stacks of paneling in the wood you like and pick out sheets that match closely enough to meet your self-set standards.

● Examine all four edges of every sheet. Quite frequently paneling is damaged by rough handling in transit, and if edges are marred, you can never make good butt joints without running the sheets through a saw to clean up the edge, thus losing coverage and very frequently throwing the job out of line with standard 16-inch-on-center stud spacing.

● Solid wood paneling is often high in defects, since a great deal of it is made from pine that is almost throwaway, except that it does make interesting paneling. Check every board when you buy solid wood for surface defects that are unacceptable. Check especially the tongues and grooves, to make sure you will not be faced with gaps between boards. Some pine paneling, of course, is sound, and most solid wood paneling of other species, such as redwood, is quite clear.

(If you are buying sheets manufactured by the rotogravure photographic process, there will be no problem with match, but there may be a problem with repeat after repeat of the same grain pattern.)

Matched moldings. Any paneling installation requires moldings to bridge the changes between wall and ceiling, wall and floor, and sometimes between paneling and some other form of wall surfacing. Unless you are working with pine and can easily pick up standard moldings made of pine, you may face problems.

Most of the so-called paneling centers and well-stocked lumberyards carry moldings to match or complement the paneling they handle. These moldings are unlikely to be made of the same wood as the sheets (particularly if you are going in for one of the exotic species), but they are finished in a way that makes them suitable companions for the paneling. Unless you are able to find molding that suits you, you may find yourself faced with the problem of painting or staining pine molding to match something as remote as avodire.

One more shopping suggestion: Ask the dealer for nails that match, or closely match, the paneling you have selected. Well-stocked outlets have special slim, ringed nails with small heads, coated with a pigment that makes them disappear when they are used with a paneling that is their color.

10

How to Panel a Room

Whether you pick one of the sheet-form paneling materials or the solid boards that come in pine, walnut, pecan, cherry, Philippine mahogany, and many other species, installation is not difficult. The boards are easy to work with from one point of view: they are light and not awkward to handle. Sheets are easy because once you have hoisted one into place and tacked it so it will stand, you have all but covered 32 square feet of wall. Strips are the easiest of all to install.

JUDGING EXISTING WALLS

Just about any residential wall, whether its original surfacing is lath and plaster, or plasterboard and plaster, or gypsum board, is suitable for the application of paneling. The only requirement is an adequately plane surface. If the surface is not only even but also in good shape structurally, it may be possible to put up paneling using special adhesives—a job often less difficult than wallpapering. If, on the other hand, the existing surface is not structurally sound,

you may be able to panel the wall by nailing into existing studs. Special paneling nails intended for installing sheets over existing walls are more than $1\frac{1}{2}$ inches long, so they will reach into studs through plaster.

As has been mentioned, many 4x8 sheet paneling materials are grooved on 16-inch centers, or otherwise treated in design so that the 16-inch nail spacing hits parts of the pattern which will conceal nail heads. Therefore, if an existing wall has its studs spaced typically, nailing is no problem. By tapping the wall, or driving nails in search of studs, you must find the answers to these questions:

Are there studs at *4-foot intervals*, to catch the edges of 4x8 sheets? Are they spaced 16 inches on center?

Can you locate the studs, even if they are not uniformly spaced?

Would it be possible to hit unevenly spaced studs without producing unacceptably visible nail heads?

Would the accommodation of existing studs give you a result that is both esthetically and structurally sound?

100

If the answer to any of these questions is "no," your best solution is furring strips. If the answer is "yes," you can expect good results by putting the sheets or strips directly over the existing wall, unless the wall is so uneven that the sheet material would lack the smooth appearance that all paneling needs.

If the wall is uneven, you should apply furring strips, with spacers back of the hollow parts of the wall, to make the face of the furring smooth and plane. If, however, the unevenness of the wall is due to loose, bulging plaster, and if the studs back of the plaster are okay, you may choose to follow a messy but effective procedure: strip the old wall-surfacing material off. How messy is this operation? Perhaps the best answer lies in the suggestion that the best tool to remove the old plaster and plaster backing is a garden spade.

ESTIMATING PANELING NEEDS

It pays to make careful calculations of paneling requirements, since dealers may not want to take back any materials that you don't use, particularly if the paneling is a special order. If you order too little, you have to take the trouble and time of getting the additional matching paneling you need.

Figure your requirements by this method:

1. Determine the length of the walls to be covered in feet, if you are using 4x8 panels, in inches if you are using 16-inch-wide strips or solid wood.

2. Divide the total footage by 4 for sheets. Divide the total in inches by 16 for strips. Divide the inches by 7 if you plan on boards. (This figure for boards will be close but not necessarily true, owing to the variations in board width.)

3. Subtract 20 square feet for standard doors, and 16 square feet for standard windows. Compute the area of fireplaces and other nonstandard openings, and subtract them from the total.

This process will give you the amount of paneling material you need—*measured laterally*. The vertical dimension depends on the height of your ceiling. Since such a large majority of ceilings are 8 feet high, standard sheet and strip lengths will do the job, as will standard 8-foot lengths of solid wood paneling. When the ceiling is a bit lower, you lose very little by cutting the 8-foot paneling to the required length, especially since the cutoff may very well fit over windows or doors.

When the ceiling is more than 8 feet, however, you have to choose between spending more (much more) money for extra-length paneling material or one of the following techniques:

Dropped ceiling. This decorating device has been used for generations, not only for handling difficult dimensions, but also as a means of giving walls extra attractiveness. All it means is that the color of the ceiling is carried down the wall for a foot or so, to a molding running around the room. Below the molding, another material completes the wall.

When you work with panels on a ceiling more than 8 feet high, use the paneling for the lower 8 feet. Run a molding along the paneling at the top. Finish it to match the paneling or paint it to match the ceiling, whichever suits your tastes.

Important: It is best to paint the ceiling and the dropped ceiling before you panel. That way, there is not chance that paint will drip on that nice new paneling. On the other hand, when you use V-board or novelty paneling of pine, you might like the effect if you paint it the same color as the ceiling and the dropped ceiling. Walls handled this way are attractive and subtle—dignified in traditional decorating schemes.

Raise the floor. Depending on the difference between ceiling height and panel length, you have some options. For example, much paneling is done with nothing but a molding at the floor—when the 8-foot dimension prevails. If the ceiling happens to be only a few inches higher than 8 feet, it is simple to run a baseboard below it, around the room. Pick a wood that matches or one that can be stained to match. Let the paneling run from the baseboard to the ceiling. Use a molding at the top and bottom of paneling. Put a shoe mold at the bottom of the baseboard.

Wainscot. When the ceiling height gives you a considerable difference over standard paneling dimensions, the solution may be "wainscot."

The wainscot is paneling that covers the lower part of the wall. Above it is paint or paper. Along the top of the wainscot there may be a shelf, or merely a molding. The shelf is often the better idea because it provides a resting place for knick-knacks or other objects the family might want to put on display.

The wainscot is traditionally popular, since it has for centuries provided the protection of paneling for the lower, and most vulnerable, area of the wall. Above it, paint or paper is high enough to be beyond the range of most dirtying and damaging exposure.

Another factor that makes the wainscot convenient is the way a sheet of paneling or strip material can be cut in half, to give you a 4-foot-high paneled wainscot. in other words, a single sheet gives you 8 feet of wall.

All in all, the best way to predetermine needs in paneling is to make a scale drawing of the walls. Let 1 inch equal 1 foot. Include all openings and other variations. Then cut a piece of paper 4x8 inches and use it to plan the way the sheets will cover the wall most efficiently, with the least amount of cutting, and with the best spacing to avoid narrow strips in corners and flanking windows. Use a guide $8x^{15}/_{16}$ inches for strip paneling.

When you have determined your needs, arrange for the paneling to be delivered *at least three days before it will go up*. Store it in the room where it will be used, lying flat on the floor. Put three lengths of wood lath or equivalent between the sheets—one near each end, and one in the middle. This allows air to circulate around the sheets, and conditions them to the environment before they are put up. That way, they will be more stable on the wall—less likely to shrink or swell unevenly.

HOW TO INSTALL FURRING

If the wall you are about to panel needs furring, the thing to keep in mind is that you are providing a *base* for the paneling, and it must be solid. Use 1x2 or 1x3 boards. Fasten them solidly to the wall. Use 8-penny common nails if you are nailing the strips to studs, special steel masonry nails if you are working on a masonry wall. These nails are specially hardened so that they can be driven into concrete block or poured concrete or brick mortar courses.

Important: If you are paneling a basement wall, and there is any history of moisture in or through the wall, be sure to cover the furring with a moisture vapor barrier. Building supply dealers handle a polyvinyl sheet in rolls that is easy to staple over the furring.

If a wall is more than 8 feet high—the standard length of most economical sheet-form materials—you can often cut pieces of any close-repeat pattern such as this brick to add to the height. Note in this installation the use of a piece of 1x4 to cover a joint and give the appearance of an old beam.

inches on center, as far as possible. Some panelers use 24-inch spacing, but there is little saving in labor or materials, and the 16-inch module is a better base for sheet, strip, or solid wood.

If you are using solid wood paneling, you do not need any vertical furring. With sheet materials, however, pieces of the furring stock must be cut to fit between the horizontals, and installed vertically. These verticals are located where the edges of the sheet material fall. This means every 48 inches for the 4x8 sheets, every 16 inches for the strips.

Because the up-and-down furring must lie beneath edges, it is necessary to plan the layout for each wall before you put the vertical furring pieces in place.

It is necessary, also, to surround windows and doors and other breaks in the wall with furring strips, to support the edges of the panels. This, as you can see, brings up a problem with door and window trim. It is relatively easy to solve, however, and will be covered later in this chapter, in the discussion of trim.

One major advantage of a furred wall is that you are no longer bound by the location of studs. The horizontals provide the basic structural requirements. The verticals do not need to be nailed to studs, since their function is to provide a back-up at the edges so the joint will resist pressure. Therefore, you can cement them in place with a squiggle of paneling adhesive. Later, when you put up the paneling, drive small nails into these pieces of furring to hold them in place permanently.

Important: When you fur out masonry walls, where there is no need for nailing into studs, you can install the furring vertically, spaced every 16 inches. With a horizontal strip at the floor and at the ceiling to catch the top and the bottom of the panel-

If there are moldings at the ceiling, they should be removed. Also, remove the baseboard and moldings at the floor. Depending on the final finish, you may be able to replace these moldings, so remove them carefully.

Spacing. Since paneling materials are produced in 16-inch modules, furring must be installed to meet the 16-inch requirements. The simplest way to do the job on a wall with studs is to nail the furring strips horizontally. Put one at the ceiling and one at the floor. In between, space them evenly 16

Furring strips spaced about 16 inches apart are essential for installing strip and solid-wood paneling. Here they are nailed horizontally to open studs on 16-inch centers.

ing, all you need to do is make sure to space a vertical furring strip at the edges of the sheets and every 16 inches between.

If the purpose of the furring is to make the wall true and plane, use spacers back of the strips wherever the wall is dished. Pick up some wood shingles to use as spacers. They are wedge-shaped, and if you slide a piece from each side overlapping in the depression, the result will be a flat nailing surface.

When you work in a situation where the studs are exposed, it is possible to provide the effect of furring strips by cutting 2x4s to length and inserting them horizontally, like fire bars, about 24 inches apart. This is particularly effective when the paneling is solid wood.

Also, if your choice in solid paneling in-

volves one of the modern ideas of installation at an angle, nothing more than the studs is necessary, since the boards cross the studs at the angle and are adequately supported.

WORKING WITH SHEET PANELING

The best practice when you put up sheets that are not tongue-and-groove is to start at the middle of the wall and work into corners. That way, you can center the pattern of the paneling and end up with equal size sheets at the corners. The first decision must be: Does a sheet of paneling or a joint between two sheets go in the middle of the wall?

To make this decision, find the center of the wall. Cut a scrap of wood 4 feet long.

Paneling a Masonry Wall

1. If you are putting up sheet paneling, nail vertical furring strips to the wall 48 inches on center. Then nail horizontal furring strips down the wall, 16 inches on center. For strip paneling, space vertical furring 16 inches on center.

2. Apply a continuous ribbon of adhesive on vertical furring strips, where the edges of the paneling rest. On horizontal furring strips, apply 3-inch strips of adhesive 6 inches apart.

3. To assure ¼-inch clearance at the top and bottom of the panel, rest the panel on shims. Use a level to plumb the panel before pressing it against the furring strips.

4. Nail the panel along the top edge to hold it in position, using nails color-matched to the panel. Then press it against the furring. Also nail the bottom edge of the panel to the furring, and drive nails in "joint" grooves or design elements where they won't show.

Starting at the center, mark off 4-foot intervals into the corner. At the corner, if you have a space more than 2 feet wide, put a *joint* between sheets at the center of the wall. If the space you end up with in the corner is less than 2 feet, start with a *sheet* of paneling centered in the middle of the wall.

If the sheets are tongue-and-groove, you must start at one corner and work across the wall, in order to hook grooves continuously over tongues. Follow the same planning procedures outlined above. Cut the less-than-full-width piece for the corner. Nail it up, and continue across the wall, using a less-than-full piece at the other corner.

When your base wall preparation and planning are finished, your next step is to plan for the arrangement of the paneling material on the wall. There are no decisions to be made when you work with solid paneling. Sheets require some planning.

True paneling experts stand the sheets up against the wall, step back, and judge their appearance. It may be that exchanging the position of a sheet or two would make the wall look better. Juggle the material around until the appearance pleases you. Consider, even, turning sheets upside down, for the best look, if they are not tongue-and-groove. Then, stack the sheets against an adjacent wall. You are ready to start paneling.

The 4x8 sheets of paneling go up either with nails, with nails and cement, or with cement only. The choice is yours—in combination with the recommendations of the manufacturers of the paneling and the adhesives. Generally, it is safe to say that the heavier plywood sheets should be nailed. Thinner, lighter, more flexible sheets of plywood and some of the hardboard sheets go up securely with the adhesives. Either

way, it makes sense to run nails across the top and bottom of the sheets, where they will be hidden by moldings. And, if the texture of the material provides nailing points where they will be hidden, there is no question that nailing plus adhesive is the best method.

Some adhesives are of the "mastic" type—quite thick. They spread out under the sheets after you apply them in squiggles along the furring strips, or in zigzags across the back and along the edges of the sheets if you are working on a nonfurred, sound wall. As they spread out, they bond to the paneling and the base. Other adhesives are somewhat in the nature of contact cement. You apply them, press the sheet in place, then pull it away for a short period of time while the adhesive cures a little. When you press the sheet back tight, it stays there.

Important: Be sure to follow the instructions on the adhesive container, and be sure to read instructions from the maker of the paneling since there may be individual specifications that differ from brand to brand.

It is highly unlikely that the sheets you use will be exactly the height of the ceiling. There will be a little space at the top of the sheet, as it stands against the wall. And, that is exactly where the space should *not* be. Raise every sheet until it is tight against the ceiling. This will make it simple to take care of trim. You may not need any trim at all at the ceiling or, at most, a run of narrow picture mold. At the floor, you can cover relatively wide gaps with a baseboard.

It is a rare wall that has no openings, and in most circumstances you'll find it necessary to do a lot of cutting around windows, door, etc. Do it this way:

● Install the last sheet before the one that must be cut out.

● Lay the next sheet on the floor with

Paneling a Flat Wall

1. To mark guidelines for applying adhesive, and to assure that panels are straight, snap a chalkline from floor to ceiling at 4-foot intervals along the wall.

2. Apply a continuous ribbon of adhesive approximately ½ inch inside the chalkline and around the entire perimeter of the area. Also apply adhesive horizontally, at 16-inch intervals, in 3-inch strips about 6 inches apart.

3. To assure ¼-inch clearance at top and bottom of the panel, rest the panel on shims. Use a level to plumb the panel before gluing.

4. Nail the panel along the top edge to hold it in position, using nails color-matched to the panel. Then press it against the wall. Also nail the bottom edge and drive nails in "joint" grooves or design elements where they won't show.

the top toward the wall where it will go.

● Carefully measure the distance from the edge of the last sheet to the side of the opening. Measure from the ceiling to the top of the opening.

● Now measure the height of the opening.

● Transfer these dimensions carefully to the sheet of paneling, mark the opening with a straight edge, and use a saw to cut out the opening.

Most often, the opening will be less than 4 feet wide. This means that you will repeat the mark-and-measure process for another sheet, cutting it out so that it will butt against the previous sheet at the top and, if it's a window, bottom.

Important: When the job you are working on will not include moldings around openings, but will have the paneling butt against the existing trim, there are special considerations in the sawing. If you work with a handsaw, make your marks *on the face* of the paneling, and cut it face up. However, portable electric saws cut on the upstroke. This means that *the top of the material being cut* may have ragged edges. For that reason, when it is important for the surface to be neat, turn the paneling, mark the back, and saw it face down.

Paneling trim. The purpose of paneling trim—as with virtually all trim around the house—is to cover joints that would be conspicuous otherwise. You can buy special moldings to cover any situation in the paneling job. If you select the kind that matches your panels, and if you use specially colored nails, the molding part of the job is simple. If you want special effects, buy moldings made of pine or other wood (whichever will lend itself best to the job) and stain or paint or antique them to meet the requirements.

Another form of paneling "trim" is metal finished to match. It comes in special forms of edging, inside corners, outside corners, joints, and other pieces.

In some cases, you may not want to use trim elements in inside corners. Instead, you run one sheet tight into the corner, and cut the mating sheet carefully for a snug fit. Some paneling experts handle outside corners by bringing both sheets exactly flush with the corner. This leaves a right-angled V which they fill with a piece of light quarter-round, appropriately finished.

Fitting paneling to irregular places. Now and then paneling must butt up against some irregular material, such as masonry, a fireplace, or a nonstandard wall. If you run into this kind of situation, you can handle it best with a process called "scribing." To do the job most accurately, follow these steps:

1. Measure from the edge of the adjacent sheet to the *farthest* point in the irregular area.

2. Cut the sheet to this exact width. In other words, cut a piece of paneling that would cover the entire area if it were as big as the widest point.

3. Stand the sheet in position, flat against the wall and up tight against the irregular surface.

4. Set an ordinary compass so that the distance between the point and the tip of the pencil is exactly the difference between the *highest* and the *deepest* points on the wall to be scribed.

5. Holding the compass with the tip and pencil exactly horizontal, ride the tip along the uneven surface, while the pencil runs along the paneling.

The result of this will be a line on the panel that exactly fits the profile of the uneven wall being matched. Cut along this profile for a perfect fit.

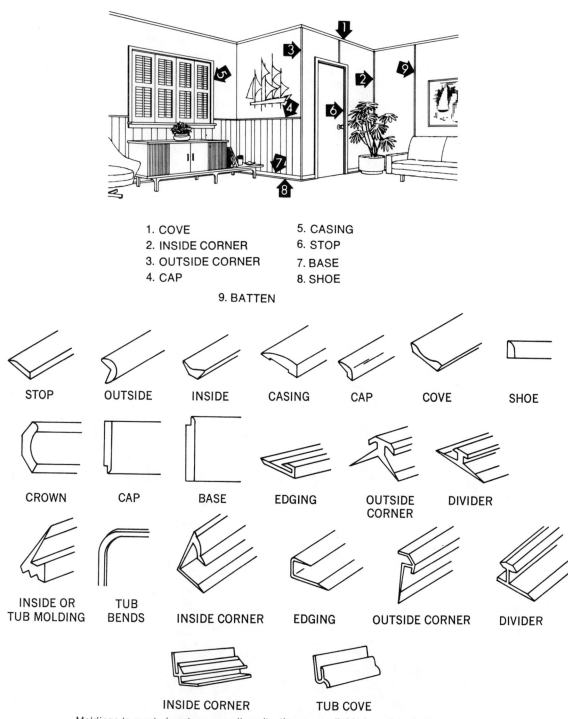

1. COVE
2. INSIDE CORNER
3. OUTSIDE CORNER
4. CAP
5. CASING
6. STOP
7. BASE
8. SHOE
9. BATTEN

STOP OUTSIDE INSIDE CASING CAP COVE SHOE

CROWN CAP BASE EDGING OUTSIDE CORNER DIVIDER

INSIDE OR TUB MOLDING TUB BENDS INSIDE CORNER EDGING OUTSIDE CORNER DIVIDER

INSIDE CORNER TUB COVE

Moldings to meet almost any paneling situation are available in metal, plastic, or wood.

WORKING WITH STRIPS

The biggest difference between strips and sheets—aside from the width—is that the strips most often have tongue-and-groove edges. This makes fitting simpler, and it eliminates the need for vertical insets in horizontal furring except for relatively flexible materials. (Read the manufacturer's instructions about furring.)

Center the paneling on the wall by the same method covered for sheet materials, but use a 16-inch stick for scribing.

Adhesives are the best method of mounting the strips on the wall, and in the majority of situations, nails are needed only at the top and bottom. If the strips have a tendency to bow out, use small nails driven into the tongue at an angle so that they do not interfere with the fit.

Techniques are basically the same as those covered in the foregoing material on sheet handling. Tongue-and-groove material must always go up with the tongued edge *leading* across the wall. Therefore, after you have used the 16-inch scribe to

Metal clips hold 16-inch-wide strips of Masonite paneling in place. The clips slip behind the leading edge of the strip, with hooks that go into the groove, over the rear lip. Two nails hold the clips in place. Then, the tongue of the next sheet slips into the groove, ready for more clips at the leading edge.

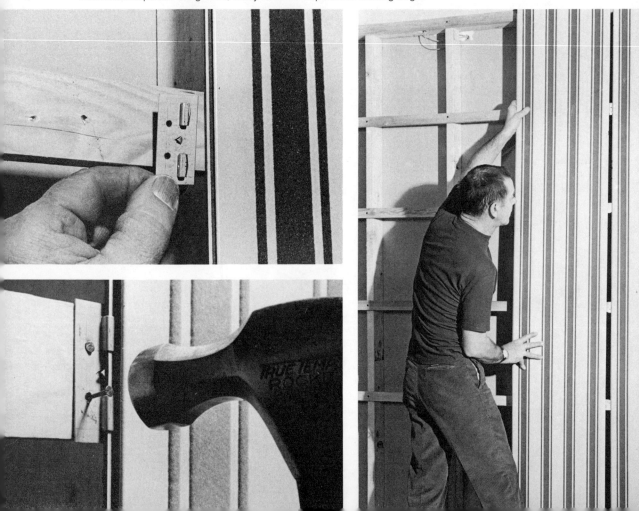

determine the width of the two strips at the corners, cut one of them to size, *ripping the waste off the groove edge.* Nail and cement that piece in place. Then work progressively across the wall to the other corner, using adhesives and nails into the tongue as may be required. Make the cutouts necessary for obstructions. When you come to the corner, cut the final strip to fit.

There is a type of strip paneling that goes up with clips instead of nails. The clips hook into the edge, and you nail them to the furring strips. The next strip hooks into the clips already in place, and you nail clips at the other edge. The system is neat, simple, and fast. There is a critical difference: the clip-mounted strips go up with the groove leading, not the tongue (see accompanying photos).

WORKING WITH SOLID WOOD

All wood intended specifically for paneling is tongue-and-groove. Therefore, it must go up with the tongue leading across the wall, since the nails go into the tongue — hidden by the groove in the next piece. If your paneling is of uniform width, you must plan to avoid ending up in the far corner with an unsightly narrow strip. Use a scribe the length of the *face* of the paneling. Start in one corner and mark your way across the wall. If this tells you that the final piece would be too narrow, rip some off the edge of the first piece to go up.

If, on the other hand, you are working with random-width paneling, start off any way you like. You can always adjust for an acceptable width for the last piece by choosing the best widths for the last few feet of the wall.

One of the most difficult phases of tongue-and-groove paneling is making sure that the boards fit as tightly as possible.

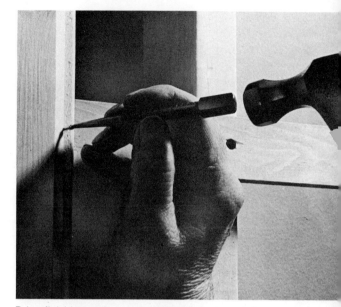

Drive finishing nails into the base of the tongue in tongue-and-groove paneling. A nailset puts the heads out of sight when the next board goes up.

Nailing at an angle into the tongued edge while you pull the board tight helps. The accompanying photographs show how a bar clamp can be used "inside out" to bring the boards as close together as possible. Also, if you are working in a situation with exposed studs, you can improvise a lever, exerting pressure on the edge of the board, backed against the closest stud, with a spacer. As you add boards, the spacer gets shorter and shorter. If you cut three or four of them from scraps of wood there is always one the right length.

Prefinishing boards. Whenever you put up tongue-and-groove paneling, two things are of extreme importance. First, the wood must be dry. For that reason you'll get the best results if you panel during the heating season, and if you season the boards for several days in the room where they will be

If it is necessary, with wide boards, to put a nail on the surface, sink it, then finger-dab a bit of water-mixed filler in the hole. When the filler is dry, sand it flush, then wipe across it—with the grain—with a damp rag.

Use a bar clamp in reverse to hold boards in tight. Put the movable stop of the clamp against the edge of the board. Hook the back of the feed against a stud. Loosen the clamp, rather than tighten it, to force the board into place.

used, allowing them to shrink before you put them up—not after you put them up.

Since it is impossible to make sure that tongue-and-groove joints will stay snug with changes in humidity, it is absolutely essential that the boards be *finished before they go up.* That way, you can apply paint or other finish to the tongue. Then, if the boards shrink, exposing some of the tongue, at least it is the same color as the rest of the wall.

It will be necessary to apply finish to the moldings and other trim, and at outside corners. The standard method of handling such corners with solid wood materials is to let one face come flush with the corner. Let the other face lap the flush surface. Use a plane to make the joint smooth. Then apply finish to the raw edge. Some panelers miter outside corners, but this is a tedious and difficult job, rarely worth the extra effort.

WORKING AROUND EXISTING TRIM

When you apply paneling to an existing wall, you are faced with the problem of trim that is already in place and not thick enough to function as trim, once furring and new paneling are in place. Two methods of handling this problem are workable.

First, you can remove the trim around windows and doors. Let the paneling come right up to the door or window frame. Then cut narrow strips of boards, just wide enough to equal the thickness of the furring-paneling combination. Nail these strips to the edges of the frames, being careful to keep the joint smooth and inconspicuous. Having thus widened the frame, you can nail the trim back in place, and finish the new elements as you do the final touch-up finishing.

Second, before you panel, nail 1x2 around the trim, on edge, so that it effectively increases the thickness of the trim to 1½ inches. This will provide an edge for the paneling to butt against. If the joint between the paneling and the on-edge 1x2 is not satisfactorily snug, install small quarter-round in the corner finished the same as the trim.

PANELING YOU MAKE YOURSELF

You can use ordinary lumber to make some of the most striking — and authentic — of all paneling. There are several forms.

Board and batten. This is a classic paneling, used both outdoors and in. It is formed by nailing boards up to 1x10 or 1x12 vertically in place, then nailing 1x2s over the joints. If you nail first on one side, then on the other, the battens keep the joint tight. Board and batten is usually painted; barn red is a traditional color choice. In some situations you may want to paint the faces of the battens a different color.

Board on board. This wall involves the same techniques as board and batten, except that the boards are spaced at a dis-

tance slightly less than the width of the boards. Then a board of the same width is nailed over the space. The result is a wall that takes good advantage of the width of the stock but without the disadvantage of edge joints.

Raised paneling. This is the most difficult of all paneling, but worth the work because of its authenticity in traditional design and its overall interesting appearance. To make it, you cut 1x12s to the proper length. Then you set a table saw or radial-arm saw to a bevel-rip position and run all the boards through on edge, producing a flat bevel on all four sides. Then rabbet the edge of a baseboard so it will accept the bottom edges of the raised panels. Cut verticals and rabbet the edges to accept the raised panels. Cut a cross rail and rabbet it to fit over the tops of the raised panels. The baseboard and verticals and cross rail are nailed to the wall, but there no nails are driven into the panels. They float free and therefore are never subject to the stresses and strains that would cause such wide boards to crack and split.

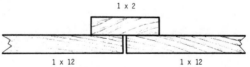

Board and batten paneling is composed of fairly wide boards — 1x12s are best — with a 1x2 nailed over the joint. The technique was originally used for exterior siding but moved indoors as a paneling variation a few years ago.

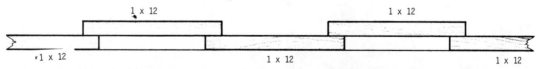

Board on board is similar to board and batten except that the boards are nailed almost their full width apart — then another board of the same dimensions is nailed over the space.

You can do an elegant paneling job using the simplest and most economical materials, as shown here in a Western Wood Products Association design. Panel the wall as covered in this chapter, using fir plywood and one A-grade face. Cut 1x4s to length to cover the vertical joints, with another 1x4 up the exact center of each sheet of plywood. Cut 1x4s the proper length to fit between these verticals at the top and bottom, with two evenly spaced 1x4s in between. Finally, cut molding as shown in the close-up photo, mitered at the corners. The finish can be stain or paint, as you wish. Important: If you finish the plywood before you apply the 1x4s, you'll eliminate the chance of shrink-and-swell revealing unfinished wood.

Installing Raised Paneling

Draw paneling design directly on the wall with chalk to see how the completed job will look. Mark the studs with arrows.

Cut the panels ¼-inch smaller than the openings and nail them to the furring. Install the moldings and you are ready to paint.

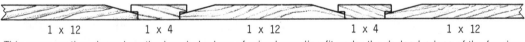

| 1 x 12 | 1 x 4 | 1 x 12 | 1 x 4 | 1 x 12 |

This cross section shows how the beveled edges of raised paneling fit under the dadoed edges of the framing members, both vertically and horizontally.

Two coats of flat enamel over a plywood sealer give just the amount of luster you need to reveal the texture of the paneling. This living room has been transformed.

Plastic laminates are now being put up in kits or units to do special jobs, such as this tub lining from Formica. All the sheets and moldings are included, ready for installation.

PLASTIC WALL COVERINGS

Many of the plastic sheet materials are attractive enough to earn a place in any decorator's dream house, but their extreme durability also earns them a place in the list of utility wall coverings. The plastics include those often referred to as Formica—a brand name. The generic term is plastic laminate, a term derived from the plastic sheets being laminated over some rigid backing.

Contact cement is the adhesive used for mounting plastic laminates. Several brands are available, and most home handymen have used them or read about them. To mount plastic laminate, brush an even coat of the adhesive on both the plastic and the base it is to adhere to. Usually one coat will do on the plastic, but it may take two coats on the base, if it is at all absorbent—as plywood would be. A good way to tell if the contact cement has been absorbed is to look at it backlighted. If the coat is dull, that is a sign that it has penetrated the base. Brush on another coat. Let these adhesive applications dry. (Check labels; some products restrict the drying time.)

When it is dry, the coating of contact cement will not stick to your fingers, or to much of anything else. It is intended solely to stick to a mating surface of contact cement. This presents a problem, since the instant one surface meets the other, it

Even in grease-and-grime situations such as the kitchen, some of today's simulations are quite workable. Brick would be a mistake in this spot, but a plastic imitation of bricks such as this one by Dacor is washable. The individual bricks, only a fraction of an inch thick, go up with mastic.

sticks. You cannot slide the plastic around to make it fit. Try one of these techniques for positioning the sheet where you want it:

● If it is possible, place the edge of the base against a "stop." This might be something as simple as putting the base on the floor or up against the wall. With the sheet raised clear, put one edge of it against the same stop. Then gradually lower the sheet in the form of an inverted arc, so that adhesion gradually creeps across the base. The arc is important since it insures even and complete contact. When the sheet is down, go over it carefully and completely

with the heels of your hands, to make sure that the two cement-coated surfaces are together.

● Another method of placing plastic laminates accurately in place requires two sheets of paper, each *slightly larger than half* the area involved. After the cement has been applied, place these sheets on the base so that they overlap in the middle. Position the laminate on the paper—to which it will not stick. When the position is correct, slide one of the sheets out until there is an inch or so of space between the two, at the middle. Press the laminate against the base along this strip. It will stick. Now you can slip the sheets out, a bit at a time, pressing the plastic hard against the base as you go.

When you put plastic laminates on a wall over a fairly large area, your best bet is to make paneling of the sheets. To do this, cement the plastic to pieces of plywood or hardboard, precut to the required size. Then, install the sheets as you would any paneling material, using adhesives. (Building supply dealers can provide detailed instructions issued by Formica.)

RIGID PLASTIC WALL MATERIALS

One of the newer plastic wall materials is a methacrylate that is extremely difficult to distinguish from marble. It is made half-inch thick for residential use. You can buy panels up to 8 feet in length, 30 inches wide. Use it for walls, or in thicker grades for bathroom lavatory tops and similar situations.

Methacrylate wall materials are handled in the same basic way as other paneling, using a mastic-type adhesive applied with a toothed trowel. The material can be worked with standard woodworking tools—drills, saws, chisels, sandpaper, etc.—but the best cutting results come from fine-toothed blades with carbide tips.

11

Modern Tiling Methods

Not many years ago, tile was considered a material for bathroom walls only, and perhaps for the backsplash area over kitchen counters. No longer. Tile was always a $4\frac{1}{4}$x$4\frac{3}{4}$-inch square, smooth, glazed, pastel-colored piece of ceramic that had to be bonded to a plaster backing. No longer.

Most homeowners today think of tile as being any of dozens of shapes and sizes and patterns in a variety of materials, suitable for use in just about any room in the house. More than that, today's tile goes on the wall with adhesives (some of them self-stick) that make the job little more difficult than pasting snapshots in your photo album. Therefore, in this chapter the wall coverings under discussion are any of those that go up in small, easily handled units.

The following is a random run-down of tiling materials.

Ceramic tile. This is still probably the most frequently used tile in the home. When properly installed, its glazed surface offers complete protection against water damage. It once came only as individual tiles, but it is now available in units of several tiles which can be handled easily and make the job go much faster. These units are backed and grouted with a rubber-like material which cuts down on the time needed for overall grouting.

The job gets even easier around tubs and shower stalls, with units that are sized to enclose stalls and tubs of various dimensions. And, the tiling operation is made still faster if you pick the kind that has peel-off, self-stick adhesive backing.

The smooth surfaces and solid colors of old ceramic tile are now augmented by a great variety in colors, patterns, and shapes. Tile sizes now include 3x6, $1\frac{3}{8}$x$1\frac{3}{8}$, 12x12, 6x$4\frac{1}{2}$, $8\frac{1}{2}$x$4\frac{1}{4}$. The oblong pieces can be used either horizontally or vertically. The colors are not always the same, bland, uniform hue that we used to see, but may vary slightly across the face of a tile, and individual tiles may vary slightly as well. Even more visual interest is provided by combining some of the plain colors with patterns or with contrasting colors.

A variety of surface shapes and textures are now available in ceramic tiles, which once came only with plain, smooth surfaces. The texture tiles are used to make patterns on their own, or in combination with smooth tiles.

As with tiling of almost any variety, tile squares are augmented by special shapes for inside and outside corners, baseboards, rounded edges, and other situations often encountered when you do a tiling job.

Mosaic tile. This is the name given to a ceramic tile that is, typically, 1x1-inch square.

It is often used for walls, backing up bathroom lavatories which may also be surfaced with the same tile. Mosaic tile comes in many different colors and the tiny pieces are sometimes used almost like artists' colors, cemented in place to form a pattern or picture of your own creation. Similar to mosaic tiles in shape and color are "quarry"

The job goes faster with units of tiles on a rubber or plastic base, such as these from American-Olean. After the mastic is spread, nine tiles go on the wall about as fast as one tile in the single system.

Ceramic wall tiles, once considered too fragile for use on the floor, are now made in grades tough enough for normal traffic. Thus, you can work out designs for walls and floors using the same tiles.

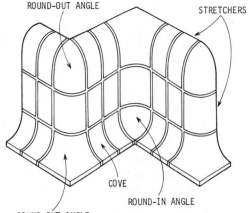

Inside and outside corners, covers for the floor-joint, and caps are standard ceramic tile elements available in colors to match standard squares.

tiles, which are solid vitreous material clear through, intended mainly for use on floors.

(Many of the ceramic tiles are glazed with sufficiently wear-resistant material to permit their use on floors, except in heavy-traffic areas. This means that you can work out tile decorating schemes with matching floor and walls.)

Plastic tile. A less expensive—and less serviceable—tile is one molded of plastic in the same size as ceramic tile with much the same appearance on the wall. It is restricted mostly to bathroom use, and is usually put up with a mastic adhesive over a base of asbestos board, which provides the water-resistance needed if leaks develop between tiles.

Molded plastic. Just about any desirable wall surface you can think of is duplicated faithfully in the form of molded plastic tile. The pieces you handle cover a couple of square feet each, weigh next to nothing, and often take advantage of self-stick adhesives. The patterns are usually those that gain their appeal through textures, such as barn boards, bricks, stones, other masonry, and many manmade patterns in geometrics, classic, and modern designs. Some of these plastic forms are duplications of wood paneling done in such intricate detail that the home craftsman could never duplicate them in real wood. These wall-covering materials are intended for living areas of the house — or areas where moisture problems are relatively small. Many of the effects possible with molded plastic tiles are possible also

with tiles molded of polyurethane foam.

The tile in molded form may be square or oblong, or even in the shape of boards.

Brick tile. Tiles the shape and size of the edge of a brick, but only a fraction of an inch thick, are available in mineral form. They come in the single color of "new" brick or in mixes of brick-red with black and white bricks that produce the popular "used" brick look. They are recommended for kitchens and other damp areas, but the bathroom is not their ideal environment. The used brick look is also produced in molded plastic individual bricks that fasten to the wall with double-faced sticky tape.

Real cork. Cork tiles come 12x12 inches, about ½-inch thick. Cemented to the wall, they provide decoration plus a pin-up board. Cork makes an excellent sound-control wall.

This well-equipped kitchen (right), with its rustic wood decor, needs an appropriate wall surface. Dacor's imitation brick is the ideal solution (below). The individual bricks go on the wall with mastic and from a few feet away look like the real thing.

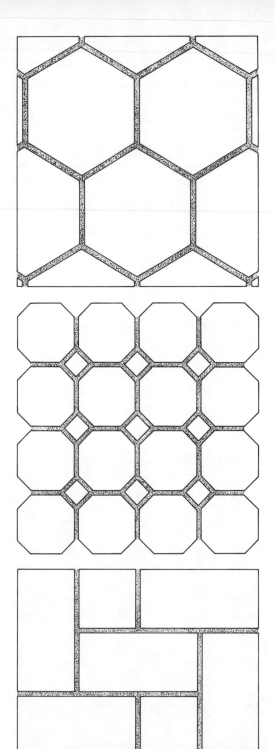

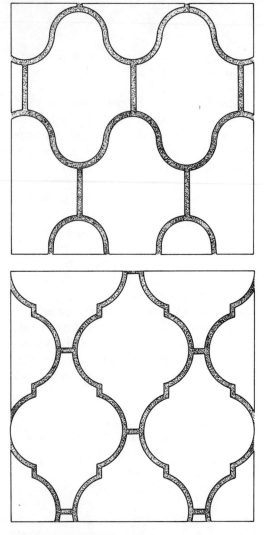

There is increasing use of tiles that are not square in the traditional manner, but in such shapes as those shown here. They interfit as simply as squares, but have extra eye appeal. Some of them are made for both walls and floors.

Metal tile. This is another imitation of ceramic tile, available in squares and in units. It is finished with a baked enamel.

Non rectilinear shapes. In addition to the square and oblong shapes of ceramic and some other tiles, there are several common nonrectilinear shapes, all of which interfit as do squares.

Hexagon and octagon are common. The hex is a true geometric shape. The octagon has eight sides, but four of them are shorter than the other four. This allows for an interfit in combination with a small square tile that meets the shorter sides. The hexagonals, of course, fit together geometrically.

There are two nonsquare shapes, called monaco, valencia, andorra, and other Spanish-style names. These tiles are combinations of straight and curved sides that interfit perfectly.

Most of the special shapes are made in the same colors and textures of other styles.

WALL CONDITION

The first consideration when you start to tile or retile is the condition of the wall. The appraisal of the wall is influenced by its location as well as the material you plan to tile with. For example, if you use one of the tiling materials preunitized in rubber backing, you can put it over a wall that is not particularly even because the rubbery backing lets the tiles follow slight curvatures. Moreover, the backing provides a built-in water resistance. If, on the other hand, you are working with standard ceramic tiles, your concerns must include the physical condition of the wall, its resistance to moisture, its reaction to adhesive materials, and its load-bearing ability.

For that reason, the most useful piece of advice is to follow the manufacturer's instructions about the base wall, the adhesive methods, and grouting methods. The Tile Council of America has established careful specifications, available from the council at 800 Second Ave., New York, N.Y. (The charge is $1.) However, individual manufacturers publish specific instructions for their individual products, free with the purchase of the materials.

New walls. If you are starting from scratch, building a new wall, you will get excellent results with a special gypsum board material specifically intended for tile back-up. U.S. Gypsum calls it Sheetrock WR. Georgia-Pacific calls it water resistant tile backer board. Your dealer may handle others.

The difference between standard gypsum board and the water-resistant type is a waterproof facing paper front and back, plus a special formulation of gypsum (plaster) for the core that has an extra water resistance. (The true terminology might not be water*proof* but the function is sufficiently water *resistant* so that you end up with a backing that will tolerate minor water leakage through the surfacing material.) To go with this special gypsum board there are special joint cements, or "grouts," equally water resistant.

In living areas of the house that are not subject to excessive moisture, ordinary gypsum board makes an ideal tile back-up. It is best to use the 1/2-inch sheets, because of their extra stiffness. Standard joint treatment is all you need.

When you build walls that must contribute structural strength and plywood is the sheet material, tiles can go right over the plywood. If there are moisture considerations, a simple solution is a thin, *smooth coating* of the waterproof adhesive over the plywood. When this coating is dry, apply the coating intended to hold the tiles in place.

Any situation calling for extra fire resistance may take advantage of sheets of asbestos board as a base for tile. The smooth, waterproof surface of asbestos board also makes it an excellent alternative base for tile in bathroom areas such as tubs and showers.

Tiling old walls. When your installation of ceramic tile is intended to provide resistance to just about everything, it must go over a wall which bears its share of the resistance burden. However, if the objective is purely decorative, all the wall must do is provide physical support for the tile.

If plaster or gypsum board is papered, the paper should come off. If they are painted, the walls should be cleaned grease-free. If the paint is glossy, it may be necessary to degloss it with a strong trisodium phosphate solution followed by a thorough rinsing. (Check the instructions on the adhesive to be used.)

When a wall presents difficult preparation problems, the quickest, easiest, and often least costly solution is a new subsurface over the old. If you use thin gypsum board (the water-resistant type when required) followed by joint treatment, the wall will be an excellent base for tile. Masonite, plywood, asbestos board, and other sheet materials can be used, but the specific aim of gypsum board for walls makes it the best bet, unless there are individual conditions or requirements that dictate otherwise.

Walls for nonceramics. Tiling materials other than ceramics or brick-veneer are usually lightweight, presenting no load-bearing problems. They are also flexible enough to follow contours of the wall unless they are extreme. Remove wallpaper. If paint is in sound condition, it will usually accept adhesives intended for the molded, light-bodied tiles, but be sure to check label instructions.

PLANNING THE TILE LAYOUT

The basic methods of planning tile layout apply to all types of tile. Although the following material discusses ceramic tile only, the procedures adapt readily to other forms of tile.

Think of a tiled wall as a series of horizontal strips, for that is the way the eye sees them, unlike wallpaper, which is seen as a series of vertical stripes. This is why the first step in any tiling job is to establish the horizontal plane.

Do this with a carpenter's level in combination with a long, straight, true board. Use the level to position the straightedge, then mark along the edge. A line level does the job, too. Hang it in the center of a tightly drawn string. Position one end of the string, then adjust the other end up and down until the level is level. Mark the positions of the ends of the string, and place a straightedge even with the marks. Draw a line along the wall. (If a wall is relatively wide, it may be necessary to do either of the above leveling jobs in two or more steps.)

Where should the level line be? This decision is based on one of the basics of tiling: start at the bottom and tile upward. Therefore, the best place for the line is at the bottom of the *lowest row of complete tile.*

Why complete tile? It may be that the baseboard or floor from which you work upward will be level. It may be that the height of the tiling will be an exact number of tiles. If both of these suppositions are true, you can use the floor as the starting place for an initial row of complete tiles. If the wall height is not an exact number of tiles, it will be best to put the fractional tile at the bottom, where it will normally be least conspicuous. If the baseboard is not level, it may be necessary to cut tiles that are progressively higher from one side of the wall to the other. Again, it is best to put this irregularity at the bottom of the wall.

Once the level has been established, nail a 1x2 across the wall, exactly level, at the point where the bottom edge of the lower row will fall. This strip will be the starting place for your tiling, and the base for lateral planning.

Positioning tile laterally. As with wallpaper and paneling, the "picture" provided by the tiling should be centered on the wall. This requires a similar centering process. Starting at one corner, stand a row of tiles on edge along the top of the 1x2 nailed level. Or, if the circumstances do not require that 1x2, stand the tiles along the floor. When you reach the other corner, if you end up with more than half a tile, there should be a *joint* between two tiles at the exact center of the wall. If you end up with less than half a tile, there should be a *full tile* on the exact center of the wall.

Important: The spacing of these tiles must be the same as it will be when they are permanently installed. If there are nibs on the tiles, this will be automatic. If not, the same spacing methods to be used in the final job must be used for the centering operation.

As might be expected, the location of tubs, lavatories, toilet tanks, and other bathroom fixtures may become factors in the orientation of tile on the wall. Such individual considerations must be worked out according to your best judgment and requirements. Also, tub walls, shower enclosures, tub levels, etc., exert influences on the spacing and planning. There is only one basic rule:

Always be sure that any *exposed edge* of tile is an original edge, not one that has been broken or cut.

A broken edge, however, may meet with trim or a bathroom fixture, or other situation where it will be caulked and sealed and where the joint is not prominent.

STEP-BY-STEP TILING TECHNIQUE

The easiest pattern of tiling for most home handymen is in the form of a "pyramid." Starting at the center of the wall, put three tiles in position, then one above the center tile. The next tile goes beside the three—another in the angle formed by two tiles, diagonally above, and another above the middle tiles, making the assembly three tiles high and four tiles wide. Continue working on the diagonal, alternating from one side to the other. That way, you are always putting tiles into position guided by the right-angle formed by preceding tiles.

Since most tile adhesives require a slight presetting time (read the labels), this process lets you work first on one side of the pyramid, then on the other, providing the required drying time.

When you reach the wall on either side, cut a tile to fit in the remaining space—unless you should be lucky enough to be working on a wall that has a full tile on each side. You must cut tiles to fit around obstructions such as the medicine cabinet, wall-mounted toilet tanks, and plumbing elements that disappear into the wall. If there will be a delay before such tiles are ready, use a putty knife or similar tool to remove the adhesive, so it doesn't harden. Then, when the shaped tiles are ready, reapply the adhesive.

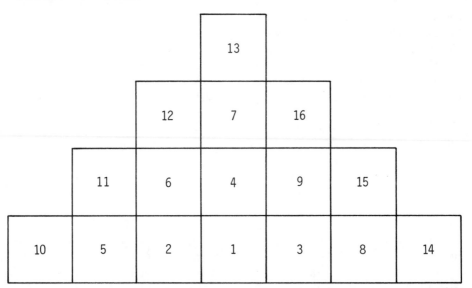

The easiest way to put up tile is to start in the middle of the wall and work in a pyramid. The tiles are numbered in the order they go on the wall. With this system, every tile can be fitted into a corner, for better alignment.

Spreading adhesive. Specific instructions for adhesive application are printed on the container. In general, however, you can expect that you will be required to spread the adhesive over a "working" size area, depending on your own speed on the job. Some adhesives will ask for some presetting time. Some will ask for the use of a toothed spreader with a specific depth and spacing of teeth.

In most cases, a proper spreader will be available at very low cost, or you may have to improvise one yourself, cutting it from a sheet of plastic or aluminum.

When spreading adhesive remember these basic points:

The adhesive must not ooze out from beneath a tile as you press it against the wall. But, there must be enough adhesive on back of the tile so that when it spreads out, it will coat the wall and the back of the tile completely.

Placing the tile in position. Most instructions for tile that goes up with an adhesive you spread on the wall call for specific application technique. They want you to put the tile up with "a sliding, twisting movement." That way, you spread the adhesive and cause it to fill in completely between the tile and the wall.

However, the sliding part of the application can cause trouble by building up an edge of adhesive in front of the leading edge. For that reason, place the tile about a half inch from the preceding tiles—no farther. It is even helpful to start with the tile closer than that; twist and slide it about a quarter inch away, then snug it up against its neighbors.

When the tile has been properly slid into place, exert firm pressure flat against it to bring it into proper contact with the wall. Some tiles, you may find, have small "lumps" on the back that prevent this pres-

Four Steps to Standard Tiling

1. Using a toothed spreader, apply a uniform coating of adhesive to the wall. Avoid thick spots but be sure to adequately coat all areas.

2. Put tile in place a fraction of an inch away from those it will butt against; then move it up snug with a twisting, sliding motion.

3. Mix the grout with water, then smear it over the applied tile, forcing it into the cracks between them. Rubber gloves and the palms of your hands work best.

4. Wipe the excess grout off the surface of the tiles, then "strike" the grout lines with the end of your finger, or the rounded end of a pencil eraser. Again, wipe off excess grout.

sure from squeezing too much adhesive out around the edges.

Close-up spacing. Side-by-side and bottom-to-top spacing are automatic with some tiling materials. They fit up together with flanges that meet in the joints where they are either invisible or made invisible by means of a form of caulk or grout.

Many ceramic tiles have little lumps or nibs on the edges which provide the spacing necessary to allow the grout to work between tiles. All you do is press each tile into its position, tight against preceding tiles, and the spacing is taken care of by the nibs. If the tile you select does not have such spacing provision, there is a simple and accurate way to handle the problem:

Use 6-penny nails, inserted point first, between the tile being set and the two adjoining tiles, near the corners. Press the new tile against these nails, both to make sure the spacing is uniform, and to hold the nails in place. Leave them there until the adhesive sets—or starts to set—then remove them with a gentle twisting motion.

HOW TO GROUT A TILED WALL

Grout is the material that fits the spaces between tiles. It serves two functions—making the wall tight, and contributing to the tile pattern by accentuating the joints. Grouting is essential with ceramic tiles, and is part of the paneling process with some other materials as well.

There are several grouting materials available from your tile dealer, who may have recommendations for your specific job. The best types for the home handyman are:

Dry-Set grout is a mixture of portland cement with additives that hold water to aid in setting. With other less sophisticated portland cement types the wall may have to be dampened before application.

Latex-portland cement grout utilizes latex mixed with portland cement and, sometimes, sand. The grout is less rigid than regular cement grout, and therefore is less likely to crack.

Mastic grout is ready-mixed and is probably the best choice for the home handyman. It is more flexible and stain-resistant than cement grouts. The Tile Council of America licenses manufacturers to make mastic grout, labeled "ACRI-FILM."

Tile centers, some paneling centers, and other outlets handle a special grouting material with a silicone base. Although this grout is ordinarily not always needed (regular materials do the job) it is often used in maintenance, should standard grout fail.

Step-by-step grouting. The grouting job, filling the joints between tiles, cannot be started until the adhesive has set and the tiles are a fixed part of the wall. Then, the general procedure is as follows—depending on the specifications provided by the manufacturer of the tile and the grouting medium.

1. Mix the grout according to instructions, unless you are using one of the pre-mixed materials. Most amateur grouters find that they have the best luck when the grout is slightly *thinner* than specified—that is, a bit more liquid. This makes it easier to smear around, as covered below. However, the grout must never be so thin that it tends to run down the wall.

2. Spread the grout over the tiled area, either with a coarse-bristle brush, or—better—by the handful. Wear rubber gloves.

3. Work across and up and down, to smear the grout into the joints between tiles. Keep in mind the need for forcing it

into the cracks to their full depth. Some grouters like to use a window squeegee as part of this operation, because it exerts a forcing pressure into the cracks and tends to spread the grout over a larger area. Also, it leaves only a thin deposit of grout over the tile surfaces, to be cleaned away.

4. Using coarse toweling or burlap or other rough fabric, wipe off the grout from the surface of the tiles.

5. Use a pencil eraser, a rounded toothbrush handle, or the end of a small dowel to "strike" the joints vertically and horizontally. This process must be followed by another treatment with the rough fabric, to remove grout "troweled" to the surface by the preceding step.

Pregrouted materials. Tiling materials that are *unitized* may not require overall grouting. The base of the unitizing not only provides a "blanket" for the multitile application, but also comes to the surface between tiles. Therefore, all you must do is apply the manufacturer's recommended edge treatment around the units.

However, some unitization involves nothing more than a cheesecloth-like backing. These require the same grouting as individual tiles.

Special-shaped tiles. When you choose tiles that are not square, you may have some special problems when you need to cut a tile. For instance, at the floor or corner — or at any other place that interferes with smooth and plane surfaces — you can cut a square tile to any width and the result is acceptable. But, if a tiling material has a definite shape and pattern, doing this may produce an ugly result. Some patterns may lend themselves to splits at other intervals, and if they do, the possibilities will be clear as you work with the tile.

Spacing between nonsquare tiles is usually easier than it is with squares. The shapes invite proper relationships, one tile to the next, and also prevent crowding one tile too close to the next.

Grouting such tiles may not be necessary, although if it is, special techniques are required, since the surfaces of nonsquare materials may be textured. Working the grout off such surfaces may require the use of special wiping techniques.

CUTTING AND SHAPING CERAMIC TILE

In spite of its thickness and cement-like nature, ceramic tile is easy to cut and shape.

Determine the cut-off point for tiles at an edge or at the floor by following these steps: (1) place a tile exactly over the last full tile in the row; (2) place another tile on top of this one, butted against the wall or floor; (3) at the free edge of this tile, mark carefully the cut-off line on the first tile. Cut along this line; the piece will fit perfectly.

If you are setting out on a major tiling project, you'll save time and labor by renting a tile cutter from your tile dealer. The

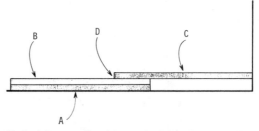

To find the cut-off point on a less-than-full-width tile, follow these steps: (1) Place tile B over tile A — the last full size to go on the wall. (2) Place tile C on tile B and move it into contact with the wall. (3) Mark tile B at the point indicated by the arrow — D. (4) Cut the tile at that point, and the piece will be a perfect fit.

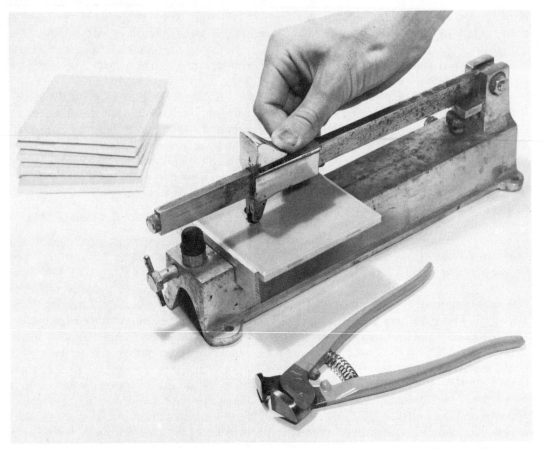

The tile cutter is a glass cutter mounted on an arm that guides it accurately across the tile, held in position on the bed of the cutter. Your tile dealer will rent you one.

cutter provides a guide for holding the tile securely and a blade that rides on an arm, making a straight cut certain. After the cutter has made its mark across the tile, you break it over the edge of the cutter table.

The job is simple, however, using a good quality glass cutter. Hold a straightedge in place across the tile and run a firm stroke of the cutter along the edge. Then place the tile so that the mark of the cutter is *directly over a piece of wire*—such as a straight length of coat hanger wire. Press down on the tile on both sides of the wire with the heels of your hands. The tile will break cleanly.

Owing to the composition of the tile, the glazed surface will be an exact edge as marked by the cutter. The ceramic base may show some toothy unevenness. Use a coarse carborundum stone, or a chunk of concrete block, to grind down any high spots that may interfere with placement.

Cutting curves. When it is necessary to cut a piece of tile to a shape instead of a straight line, follow these steps:

1. Determine the shape of the cutout and mark it on the tile. The best instrument for marking is a fine tip felt pen.

2. If the cutout must be made inside the edges of a tile—as it would be if you were cutting a hole for a plumbing run—break the tile in two, using the glass cutter as explained above.

3. With the glass cutter, carefully run around the shape to be cut. You may find it best to make a light run first and let it guide a second cut with full pressure. despite admonitions you may have heard never to make two passes with a glass cutter.

4. Use a tile nipper (available on rental) or a tough pair of slip-joint pliers and gradually nibble away the unwanted part of the tile. You will find that the pressure of the tool crumbles the ceramic, making it easy to achieve the desired shape if you work in very small bites.

5. If you had to break the tile to make the cutout, put the two pieces in place, forcing the break back tight together. Be careful not to get mastic adhesive in the break; it will hold the joint apart.

SOME POINTERS ON MOLDED PLASTIC

Some molded plastic tile materials are rectangular, some have interfitting ends, some are in the form of panels and stiles and crossmembers. These factors, combined with occasional patterns that are intended to look entirely random, make it necessary to anticipate certain problems.

To begin with, many of the molded tiles are designed with heavy textures. The deepest depressions in the texture hit the wall. It is standard for the design to allow all the edges to hit the wall. Back of other areas there is air space. As a consequence, when you cut molded plastic tiles, you may end up with an edge that has no support in back of it. When this happens in an inside corner, there is no problem. If it happens on an exposed corner, check with the dealer for special moldings.

Cutting molded plastics is simple. All you need is a pair of heavy shears. You may run into trouble when you center the overall tiled "picture" on the wall, because of the amount of the individual tile pattern that is left at the edges. Many of the designs must be cut exactly in the middle, or the result looks odd. When you meet this problem, an easy and attractive method of handling it is with strips of wood in the corner, ripped to the proper width to permit cutting the less-than-full tiles in the corner exactly in half. Paint or stain the corner boards to go with the tile.

Since these tiling materials are relatively new, and since they are entirely different in form and in handling, most of the manufacturers have elaborate instruction sheets, excellently illustrated, with full technical information.

Using Wall Space Effectively

12

Most walls in the house are intended as partitions between one living area and another, or between indoors and outdoors. There are, however, many types of walls which serve those functions, but go beyond the basic duty and provide additional utility. Most of them require nothing more than the addition of functional features. Some require special construction. Some obtain their special functionality through the use of special surfacing materials. Some can be put into use with nothing more than ingenious hanging methods. Some require the engineering of special acoustical controls. Yet, none of them present problems beyond the abilities of the average home handyman.

UTILITY STORAGE WALLS

The typical wall in a house is about 5 inches thick and represents a complete waste, insofar as space is concerned. Every foot of that wall takes up almost 3 cubic feet of space. You can't remove the wall, of course, but there are ways of modifying it

so that it *provides* space, rather than wasting it.

The wall is hollow. Inside it are, almost always, 2x4 studs. Their purpose is to provide a backing for the wall surfacing and often to provide support for floors above.

There would be just as much physical support in ⁵/₄x8s. The depth of the wall would increase from $3^1/_2$ inches (the width of a 2x4) to $7^1/_2$ inches (the width of the ⁵/₄x8s). If you are building a wall, why not use the wider stock — and let the "studs" support shelves? You could even face half of the wall on one side, half on the other, and provide storage on both sides.

Building shelves along an existing wall would give you the same storage space, if the size of the room would allow the 10 inches or so of floor space the shelves would occupy. A good deal of such space would not be lost of you built the shelves from a level of 4 feet — more or less — up to the ceiling. And, if 5 inches would not make a difference, you could take the facing off the wall and let the shelves extend into the wall as far as the back side of the facing on the

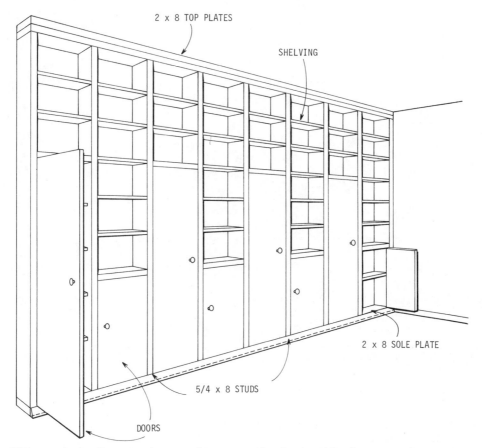

While standard wall construction occupies space, rather than providing it, you can often construct walls with adequate strength and a great deal of storage space. An example is this wall of $5/4$x8 studs that provide more shelf area than would standard 2x4's as well as room for closed storage areas.

other side. If appearances are critical, cement thin plywood or hardboard to that facing and paint it.

Mounting shelves on an existing wall or one that is built from scratch is simplified by special shelf brackets and mounting fixtures sold by lumberyards and hardware stores. They can be screwed to studs or to plaster walls (with proper anchors) and brackets can be inserted at any level. Brackets come in several lengths, to accommodate shelves of different widths.

HANG-UP WALLS

A great deal of storage is possible on walls built to accept hangers. The most common is the wall made of perforated hardboard. There are hangers (about 100 different sizes and forms) that fit in the holes and support anything you might want to hang on a wall.

Although the original—and most common—use of perforated hardboard is in functional areas, the sheets are now being

Wall system converts otherwise wasted space into a functional and decorative storage area. This set of System Cado units includes a desk, bar, chests, shelves, and room for a TV and hi-fi.

Some Masonite paneling materials fasten to the wall with steel supports which also form the anchors for shelf brackets. The result is a wall of shelves with no distracting verticals.

made in a variety of textures, prefinished, and otherwise decorative faces. The hangers, too, are attractive enough in many forms to be part of the decorative scheme of playrooms, bedrooms, kitchens, and other informal parts of the house.

INSULATED WALLS

Walls may be insulated for two reasons: to cut down the transmittal of heat through the wall or to cut down the transmittal of noise through the wall.

Thermal insulation. It is not simple to insulate existing walls against heat loss. One method often recommended is the use of insulation in the form of small particles—

Hangers of dozens of shapes and functions are available for use with perforated hardboard walls. These are some of the simplest and most universally useful. Also, your dealer can provide complete shelf units most interesting because their welded-rod design adds to the open feeling that is at its best displaying potted plants.

Perforated hardboard in decorative patterns and finishes is appropriate for hanging walls in kitchens and other areas of the house that are lived in.

such as styrofoam beads or a product called Vermiculite. To load an existing wall, you cut through the surfacing material just below the ceiling in each stud space, and pour granules until the space is full. This is a good method—unless the wall is built with fire stops crosswise between studs, as is often the case. With stops in the wall, the granules cannot drop to the floor to fill the cavity completely. It may be worth the bother to cut openings below the fire stops, too, depending on the heat loss problem.

Another method of handling existing walls against heat loss is with sheets of styrofoam. The sheets, cemented to the wall, contribute greatly to heat control. They increase the thickness of the wall by about 2 inches—presenting problems accommodating trim around doors and windows. You can "thicken" the trim to take care of the situation by methods covered in Chapter 10.

If your decision is to use foam, it is often possible to cement the insulation to an existing wall that is not in bad shape. Then, it is often recommended that paneling or other surfacing material be applied directly over the insulation with adhesive. Another method is to combine the insulation with furring strips between the sheets, then fasten the surfacing material to the furring. Since the foam is standard in strips 24 inches wide, horizontal application would provide nailing for paneling every 2 feet.

Any construction of outside walls around your home should include insulation. Most convenient are batts, wide enough so that they are snug fit between studs, and with flanges so they can be stapled to the studs. The batts should have an aluminum or other facing which acts as a moisture-vapor barrier and a heat reflector. How thick the batts should be depends on the climate where you live—a question your building supply dealer can answer.

Noise control. When the job of a utility wall is to control noise, it can function in one or both of two ways.

● Control of noise may be required *in the room* where the noise originates. This would be the situation in a family activity room where the goings on create noise that the family might like subdued.

● Control of the noise that originates *on the other side of the wall* may be required. This situation exists where the family wants to confine the noise of that family room, instead of letting it spread throughout the house, or where street noises must be quieted down, or where the racket of a workshop may need to be confined, or, often most important of all, when a special area as a sickroom or a nursery must be insulated from the noise of the rest of the house.

Control within a room is a matter of cutting down the way noises bounce from wall to wall, ceiling to floor. Most of the responsibility for control rests with the ceiling, which is the largest area in the room, and most often quite smooth and reflective. (For the contribution of ceilings to noise control, see Part III.) Floors bounce noise, too, but they are often covered with rugs or carpeting that absorb much of the noise. And that is the secret of sound control within a given area: provide a surface that absorbs the noise.

None of the standard wall materials, such as paneling, gypsum board, or plaster, help much with sound control. What is needed is a soft textured face. Fabric is ideal. A wall covered by a drapery absorbs noise.

In some situations, you might find acoustical tile intended for ceilings extremely effective in making walls contribute their share. The textures and patterns of these tiles, usually 12x12 inches square, make an attractive wall surface. However, since they are not resistant to physical damage, you

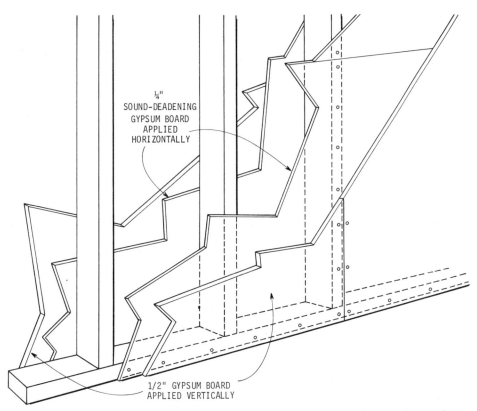

¼"
SOUND-DEADENING
GYPSUM BOARD
APPLIED
HORIZONTALLY

1/2" GYPSUM BOARD
APPLIED VERTICALLY

To build a wall that resists transmission of sound, use the technique shown here, two layers of gypsum board on each side. For existing construction, addition of another layer of half-inch gypsum board over that already in place increases the sound barrier.

might want to put them above a wainscot of a tougher material, perhaps 4 feet up the wall. With the floor under control by means of rugs or carpeting, and with the ceiling covered with acoustical tile, the use of the acoustical material on the upper half of the walls would make a tremendous difference.

Through-the wall. Sound travels through a wall by setting up vibrations in the surfacing on one side, which travel through the intrawall space and set up vibrations in the surfacing on the other side. In addition, the vibrations travel through the wall using the studs as a means of transportation. Both

means of sound transmission can be controlled by rather simple means.

The ability of a substance to *interrupt the flow of sound* depends to the greatest degree on *mass*—weight, pure and simple. It is harder to make a heavy material vibrate than a light material.

One of the simplest and easiest ways to cut down on sound transmission is to double the thickness—i.e., the weight—of the surfacing. If you combine mastic adhesive with nails and put up a layer of half-inch gypsum board on the wall, you add enough weight to cut down a lot of the noise. Do this on both sides of the wall and the reduc-

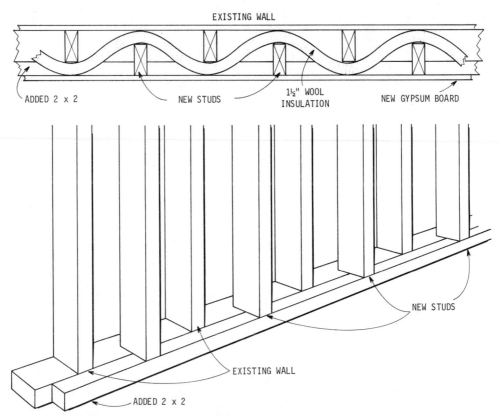

EXISTING WALL

ADDED 2 x 2   NEW STUDS   1½" WOOL INSULATION   NEW GYPSUM BOARD

NEW STUDS

EXISTING WALL

ADDED 2 x 2

When there is need for control of both sound and heat, the system sketched here is useful. The wool batts snaked through the studs do not, however, contribute much to sound control—only to heat.

tion is doubled. Your building supply dealer can supply you (probably on special order) with special sound-control board that has more mass than regular materials.

The second method of increasing the ability of a wall to intercept the flow of sound is to break the continuity. This is done quite easily and economically with the "staggered stud" system. As you know, a standard wall is composed of a 2x4 sill on the floor with 2x4 studs running vertically to a 2x4 plate at the ceiling. In the staggered stud system, the sill and the plate are 2x6's instead of 2x4s. The studs are 2x4's, but there are twice as many of them. On one side of the wall, they are spaced 16 inches on center with the edges flush with the front edges of the sill and plate. On the reverse side, they are centered between the other studs, 16 inches on center, flush with the other edge of the 2x6 sill and plate.

Thus, when the surfacing material goes on, it is not directly connected with the surfacing on the other side of the wall, and the sound cannot be transmitted directly through the studs. Construction of a new wall that takes advantage of this principle is simple, merely using the 2x6s and the extra studs. The job can be done with an existing wall, too.

Remove the wall surfacing from one side of the wall. Spike 2x2s at the edge of the plate and the sill, nailing both into those members and into the floor and ceiling joists if they run in the right direction.

You end up with a sill and plate equivalent to a 2x6, and with half of the studs already in place. Now install studs *between those in the wall,* with the edges flush with the forward edge of the 2x2. Be sure to maintain 16-inch on-center spacing. You're ready to put new surfacing material in place. This method of sound control is particularly handy when you are working on an exterior wall, since all of it can be done on the inside of the wall.

(Some builders snake insulation material through the wall, weaving it in front of the back studs and in back of the front studs. This reduces the transmittal of vibrations a bit more, although the mass of the insulation materials is not enough to have a tremendous effect. The value is greater in heat control.)

If the need for cutting down sound transmission is great enough, you can add *double-layer surfacing* to the offset stud construction.

When a wall that is guilty of sound transmission includes a door, it must be treated, too. A great deal of noise passes through an ordinary door, and a great deal more passes around it. Plain old weatherstripping around the door helps. If the door is light in weight, you can cut down on its sound transmission by cementing a sheet of quarter-inch asbestos board to one or both surfaces. If the noise load is light, a sheet on one side may do the job, but be sure to put it on the side where the noise originates.

Windows let in a lot of noise from the outside, but it can be cut down by leaving the storm windows in year-round, and making sure that weatherstripping is doing its job. Heavy curtains or draperies over windows, where light and visibility are not important, serve as a sound absorber.

TRANSPARENT-TRANSLUCENT WALLS

There are times when a wall — or a room divider — serves its function best if light can pass through it, bringing some illumination to the other side. Sometimes it is important to have a degree of visibility, too.

Translucency is easiest to achieve with special plastic panels lumber dealers or panel centers handle or can order for you. These panels come in a variety of colors, patterns, and textures. When the light is on *this side* of them, they look like solid paneling material with an attractive pattern and gloss. When the light is on the *other side,* the pattern is silhouetted and accentuated.

These materials are framed into room dividers in much the same way as you would frame glass, using moldings. They can also be used to replace glass in actual windows where their decorative light transmission would be appropriate and visibility is unimportant.

A useful see-through material is "filigree" board, a form of hardboard stamped with decorative holes. It can be handled and finished like any hardboard, but most conveniently with spray equipment. The same type of material is also made of plywood.

CEDAR UTILITY WALLS

A utility wall faced with aromatic red cedar is becoming increasingly popular. The walls are, of course, in a closet, and the cedar is used on ceilings and floors too. The purpose is to protect clothing against

Useful and attractive way to provide a see-through wall is by means of an actual opening, fitted with a flower box and plants.

Translucency without transparency is the objective of walls such as this, using Filon plastic in combination with cut-out materials.

In a sliding-door setup, translucent plastic provides complete privacy — or complete open view — between areas of the house.

moths. You can line any closet in the house with aromatic red cedar, available at building supply dealers. Be sure to put the cedar on the back of the door, too. No finish goes on the cedar; its value comes from the odor of the wood, which must not be sealed off. If, after a period of time, the aroma fades, go over the cedar surfaces with medium sandpaper, to cut away the natural "sealant" on the surface of the wood.

Since more cedar means better moth repellancy, make any shelves, drawers, etc., in the closet out of aromatic red cedar. Full information on cedar closets is available from:

The Aromatic Red Cedar Closet Lining Mfg. Assoc.
Suite 3906
221 North La Salle Street
Chicago, Illinois 60601

HOW TO HANG THINGS ON WALLS

At its simplest, hanging something on a wall may mean nothing more than locating a stud and driving a nail into it. Things get more complicated when you can't take advantage of the stud, but must hang something on a wall that may be only a single layer of gypsum board.

There are several special fasteners used for hanging things on a thin wall, most of them common and well-known.

The standard *picture hook* is a metal hook with its own sharp-pointed nail, positioned in the hook so you drive the nail into the wall at a downward angle. The hook can be used for hanging relatively flat objects that are quite heavy, provided the *stress is down—not out.* Outward stress tears the hanger from the wall. If the wall is made of thin gypsum board, many people use two hangers for heavy objects, spaced several inches apart so that they share the load.

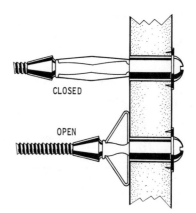

The "Molly screw" slips through a hole drilled in plaster or gypsum board. Then, as the screw is tightened, the sleeve flares inside the wall, and thereby making a solid fastening.

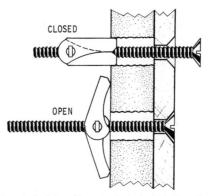

The toggle bolt has flip-out wings, held in flared position by springs. To use the bolt, hold the wings together and slide them through the hole in the wall. Inside, they spring apart, and form a "nut" for the screw to turn in.

The plastic anchor is embedded in a hole drilled in gypsum board or plaster. A screw of the proper size is then threaded through the hole in the object to be attached to the wall and screwed into the anchor. The pressure of the screw expands the anchor.

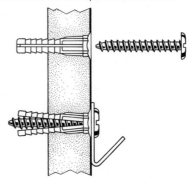

Since picture hangers cost very little, there is no reason why the two-hook technique should not be used whenever the object is heavy.

"Molly screw" is the name given to a hanger used to fasten things to the wall—not merely to hang them. This special device is a screw that runs the length of a tube before it reaches the nut it screws into. The tube is slit along the sides. To use it, drill a hole the size of the tube. Slide the molly through the hook on the object being hung and through the hole in the wall. Holding it firmly against the wall, drive the screw. When you do this, the nut at the far end is drawn toward the back side of the wall material, flaring the tube. When the screw is tight, the tube has formed a "snowshoe" on the back of the wall, providing a hanger that is quite strong, since it would have to break out a piece of the wall material an inch or so in diameter in order to come loose.

Toggle bolts are another form of fastener that "snowshoe" inside the wall. These bolts have a pair of arms mounted around the nut, with springs that make them flare apart. After you drill through the wall, compress the wings and shove the unit through the wall. Inside the wall, the wings flip open, and when you drive the screw they provide support. Toggle bolts are used for relatively heavy hanging objects.

Plastic and lead anchors are made for attaching things to solid masonry or plaster walls. They can also be used in hollow walls if the surfaces are fairly thick. All of them function on the basis of expansion.

To drill into masonry, use a carbide-tipped bit in an electric drill or a "star" drill and a hammer. Make the hole the same diameter as the fastener and a little deeper than its length.

Lead anchors are considered strongest for masonry, your best choice when you are fastening something that weighs a lot and produces forward as well as downward stresses.

Part II

FLOORS

13

How Floors Are Built and Maintained

There are only two kinds of floors in residential construction—suspended and slab. The slab is poured on the ground. The suspended is built over a basement or crawl space—or over a lower floor, in which case it is both floor and ceiling. Of the two, suspended floors are many times more numerous than slab floors—although slabs have been increasing in recent years.

ELEMENTS OF WOODEN FLOORS

Wooden floors that are suspended over space are constructed of five elements: joists, headers, bridging, subfloor, and flooring material.

Joists. The floor is supported by heavy planks, placed on edge 16 inches apart—in which position they have their greatest resistance to bending. The joists may be 2x6s, 2x8s, 2x10s, or 2x12s. The width

depends on the span—the distance they must bridge. The required width is set by local building codes, usually based on recommendations of the federal housing authority. If you are building a floor, any good lumber dealer will be able to recommend proper widths for the span. Many builders prefer to use joists the next width up, as a means of insuring a firm floor, not just a good enough floor.

The ends of first-floor joists rest on supports which may be the basement wall or other foundation. When the span is too great to be bridged by single joists, there is a girder down the middle of the span, and joists run from the walls on both sides to the girder in the middle. At the girder, the joists lap each other where they meet. The girder may be a steel I-beam or a wooden 6x6 or 8x8 or a beam made by spiking three or four 2x6s or 2x8s together. It is supported at the ends on the foundation, and

145

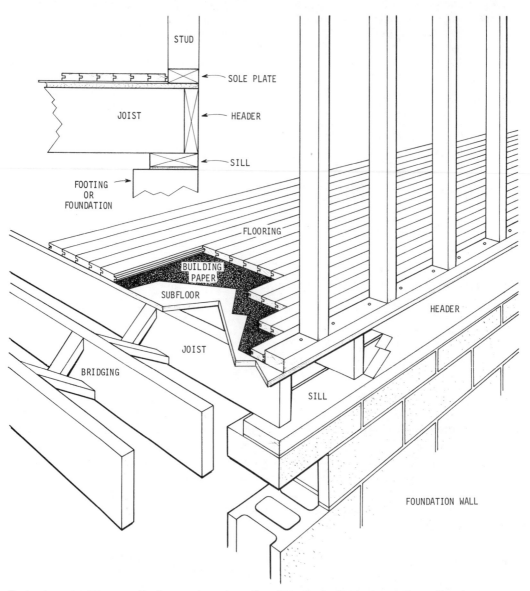

STUD

SOLE PLATE

JOIST

HEADER

SILL

FOOTING
OR
FOUNDATION

FLOORING

BUILDING PAPER

SUBFLOOR

JOIST

HEADER

BRIDGING

SILL

FOUNDATION WALL

Basic elements of floor construction are shown here. The *sill* is attached to the foundation wall and acts as a support for the *joists*. The *header* is spiked to the sill and into the ends of the joists. The *sole plate* goes on top of the *subfloor*.

usually has a column or two spaced evenly to support it in the middle.

Second-floor joists are supported at one end by the outside walls of the house, and at the other end by interior partitions. Or, in some cases, both ends may be supported by partitions, depending on the layout of the house. In most cases the shortest possible span is used, in the interest of the most solid floor. The short-span principle is a great aid when you are attempting to determine the "run" of joists when they are cov-

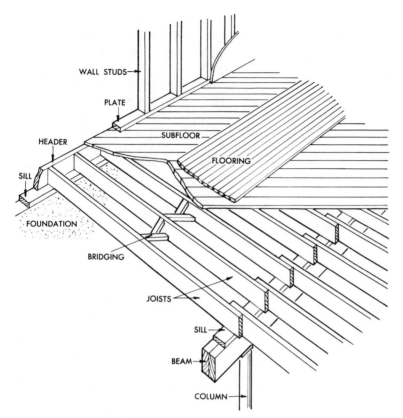

WALL STUDS

PLATE

HEADER

SILL

FOUNDATION

BRIDGING

JOISTS

SILL

BEAM

COLUMN

SUBFLOOR

FLOORING

This drawing shows how joists lap over a beam when the span is great, how subflooring is laid diagonally, and how strip flooring is layed across the joists.

ered up by floors and ceilings: most of the time, the run will be across the narrow dimension of the room involved.

Since a first floor usually must support walls, some thought must be given to the handling of joists along lines of support. If the standard 16-inch joist spacing puts a joist under a wall, the standard procedure is to double that joist by spiking two members together. Builders make sure to maintain one of them in the 16-inch-on-center progression.

If a wall must rise along a line that is parallel to the joists but not over a joist, common procedure is to space "solid bridging" between the two joists the wall comes between. Solid bridging is planks of the same

dimensions as the joists, cut for a snug fit between joists, and spiked in place with 20-penny spikes through both joists into the ends of the bridging.

Headers. Wherever joists rest on basement walls or foundation, they are held in vertical position by headers. These are 2-inch planks spiked across the ends of the joists. The headers as well as the joists are fastened to the sill, a wooden member running along the top of the masonry wall.

Bridging. This part of floor construction is one of the most important and least understood of all elements in residential construction. Bridging is the X's of 1x4s

147

(sometimes 1x3s) between the joists. Each crossbar of the X is nailed to the top of one joist and to the bottom of the joist next to it.

Ideally, bridging should be installed by two people. One works below the floor, the other above it, after the joists are in place. The man below nails the lower end of a length of 1x4 at the bottom of the joist, with the other end sticking up through the floor, resting on the adjacent joist. The upper man saws the 1x4 off, flush with the face of the joist. It falls into place, flush with the upper edge, where he nails it in place. Meanwhile, the man below has done another bottom-edge nailing job, and it goes on, over and over again.

The purpose of bridging is to increase the rigidity of the floor, which it does by tending to convert each pair of joists into a "beam" by distributing stresses up and down and laterally. In a sense, the bridging functions in the same way as truss construction in steel girders. That is why it is important for bridging to be properly fitted and securely nailed in place.

Subfloor. In early home construction, the subfloor was the floor. Boards were nailed to the joists and that was what you walked on—cushioned perhaps by a braided rug or two. Later, if the family could afford it, the subfloor was covered with a fancier material. That is basically the way the two-layer floor goes together today.

In contemporary construction, a subfloor may be individual boards—tongue-and-groove or half-lap—or it may be plywood. It is standard practice, when boards are used, to nail them diagonally across the studs. That makes it possible, later on, to put down flooring with no chance of joints in the two layers coinciding and producing weak spots.

Plywood subflooring comes in 4x8 sheets, $\frac{5}{8}$ of an inch thick, with tongue-and-groove on the long edges. The 4x8 dimension coincides with the 16-inch spacing of floor joists.

Sheets should be installed with the long dimension across the joists. That way, the ends meet over a joist for a firm joint. The edges meet, tongue and groove, for a firm running joint from joist to joist. Experts avoid letting end joints fall along the same joist by cutting sheets in half and starting every other row with a half-sheet.

Nailing calls for the extra holding power of ringed nails or other special large-headed nails that lumber dealers sell. They go every 6 inches along the ends resting on joists and every 12 inches along joists from edge to edge.

With so many construction phases now involving adhesives, it could be expected that the plywood industry would devise a glue-down method of installing subflooring. The system recommended by the American Plywood Association involves a special adhesive put up in dispenser tubes. It reduces nailing, increases strength, and reduces construction problems. Complete details for its use are given in a leaflet produced by the American Plywood Association, 1119 A Street, Tacoma, Washington, 98401.

Flooring. There are dozens of materials used for the flooring itself. Selection depends on appearance, resistance to wear and tear, and the work involved in installation. These are all discussed in the following chapter.

Underlayment. Except for full-thickness strip flooring, most floor surfacing materials require a pretreatment called "underlayment." This is a layer of quarter-inch hardboard, plywood, or particle board nailed over the subfloor. It goes down with *special ringed flooring nails* called "sinker nails." These nails are not only ringed for extra holding power, but they also have thin-edged heads that can be easily driven flush and smooth with the surface. They must be smooth and flush, since the purpose of underlayment is to provide a surface as smooth and texture-free as possible. Any roughness is likely to show through any of the flexible floor surfacing materials.

The special smoothing function of underlayment is essential if the subfloor is board-by-board. When you put a new floor over an old one, it bridges warping and other irregularities that cannot be tolerated under today's smooth flooring surfaces.

RESIDENTIAL MASONRY FLOORS

The floor in the basement, and usually in the garage, is a concrete slab. In recent years a great many entire houses have been built on slabs poured on the ground, with no basement — not even crawl space. The slab rests on a carefully prepared base and is usually surrounded by a footing that runs below the frostline — providing the actual foundation for the house. An excellent feature of much on-slab construction is the installation of heating elements in the slab, providing the highly efficient "floor radiant" heating. In preparation for pouring a slab, contractors create a level base, composed of gravel or crushed stone. This material is well tamped and made as firm as possible. Over it, the concrete slab is poured. But, before the slab goes down, utility runs are installed, which will be embedded in the concrete. Such runs would include the radiant heat components. Another important element is a moisture-vapor barrier between the base the the slab — usually in the form of heavy plastic film. This film prevents the penetration of moisture through the slab to the interior surface,

The elements of a poured slab floor are shown here: the foundation of concrete blocks; the pastic sheet that forms the moisture vapor barrier; the wire mesh that provides reinforcement; and the concrete that is poured and spread.

where it would cause early decomposition of flooring.

Although concrete slabs that must carry relatively light loads do not require reinforcement, it is considered good practice to use welded-wire mesh reinforcement in residential slabs. The common procedure is to pour and rough-spread a layer of concrete, then place the reinforcement mesh over this layer—following immediately with the remainder of the slab. Another method is to lay the mesh over the vapor barrier, then pour the cement and lift the mesh with a hook after the cement is poured, but before it is troweled. This reduces greatly the chance that the slab may crack or fissure.

The typical home handyman may, at one time or another, be called upon to repair concrete slabs that have cracked or scaled. He may from time to time be faced with the job of surfacing a slab with a flooring material. But only the very handy homeowner (with a few equally handy friends) should attempt to pour a slab of any size that must be professionally smooth and level.

REPAIR AND UPKEEP OF FLOORS

Nothing very serious ever goes wrong with the floors of a well-built house. But they do sometimes sag—and the repair techniques are covered on the following pages. Sometimes boards or other surfacing materials get so bad that they must be replaced. Such replacement is also explained. Sometimes—even *often*—floors squeak.

Floors that squeak. When a floor squeaks, it means that some structural members have given way slightly, allowing two pieces of flooring or subflooring, or both, to rub together. The first step in eliminating the noise is to pinpoint its location. Have a helper activate the squeak while you put an ear close to the floor. If the problem is on the first floor, with a basement or crawl space beneath it, you may be able to locate it exactly by listening below, and watching for motion in the subflooring as weight changes on the floor above. It may help, also, to lay your fingers gently across the floorboards, in search of vibrations that cause the squeak.

The easiest way to eliminate the squeak is with a lubricant. Use ordinary oil, or try one of the spray lubricants or powdered graphite. Fill the crack. Move around on the floor, providing the same action that causes the squeak. If the noise goes away, you've licked the problem. Let the oil soak in for a few minutes, then wipe up the mess.

If the squeak if caused by floorboards rubbing against subflooring, the oil-can method may not work. In this case, apply the weight that causes the squeak, or have a helper stand there. While the weight is on, drive two nails through the floor at an angle—in the manner of toenailing—one slanting one way, the other in the opposite direction. If possible, they should hit a joist. Set the nails below the surface with a nail set, then fill the holes with matching wood plastic or with plain wood plastic, followed by stain to match the surrounding wood. (Since flooring wood is hard—usually oak or maple—you may have to drill small holes to avoid bending the nails as you drive them.)

If the floor still squeaks, you may have to go at it from below. Try tapping shingles into any spaces between the subfloor and the joists. This will eliminate movement which may be causing the noise. Check to see if structural members are rubbing together. If they are, drive spikes through them, to eliminate the movement.

Another sure way to eliminate friction between the floor above and the subfloor below is with screws. After you have es-

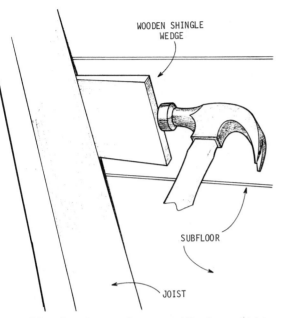

WOODEN SHINGLE
WEDGE

SUBFLOOR

JOIST

When there is space between subflooring and joists, causing squeaks, fill the space by tapping shingles gently into the opening. Hold them in place with brads driven up into the subfloor.

tablished the squeaky area, drive screws up from below, through the subfloor into the flooring. Pick No. 10 or heavier screws that are a quarter-inch *shorter than the combined thickness* of the subfloor and flooring. The screws will be hard to drive into hardwood flooring, unless you drill holes with a device like the Screwmate, which is available to match all standard screw sizes.

You can use screws from the top side of the floor, too, if you countersink them. Use a plug cutter, available at good hardware or woodworking shops, to cut cross-grain plugs for the screwhead holes, to make them as inconspicuous as possible.

Floors that sag. A sagging floor can be nothing more than a nuisance — or it can be an indication of a serious structural shortcoming. All floors sag — except cast slabs

on a well-prepared base. Gravity is at work on them at all times. New construction begins to drop between major bearing points while the workmen are walking off the job. Sooner or later, the sagging reaches the point of final resistance and the floor stabilizes. Later, an extra-heavy load or a shift in support or the failure of a supporting member may cause further drop.

Correcting the sag may be easy — or difficult — or just about impossible. It depends on what causes it and where it it located. When a first floor sags and there is space beneath it, there is virtually no problem. If it is a second floor, with living area beneath it, repair may be a major job.

The first step is to locate the effective center of the sag. You can do it with a golf ball — if the sag is enough so the ball will roll to the center. Another way is with a long straightedge placed across the sag. The deepest point is the effective center.

Repair involves two stages. First, you must jack up the sag to level (or a bit higher than level), anticipating a slight return of the sag when the jacking device is removed. Second, you must reinforce the structural member that is permitting the sag.

Just about always, this will be a floor joist, or two or more joists. Fixing things is simple enough if you can get under the floor in a basement or crawl space, but if the sag is in a joist that is also a ceiling joist, repair will require stripping off the ceiling material, except in the rare situation which would allow the installation of a column or post or partition in the room below the sag.

Jacking techniques. You can rent a house jack from building supply dealers — either a screw jack or a hydraulic, which is easier to use and provides greater hoisting power. Or, if the sag is to be eliminated by means of a permanent column, the easy answer is a column-jack (often called TelePost). This

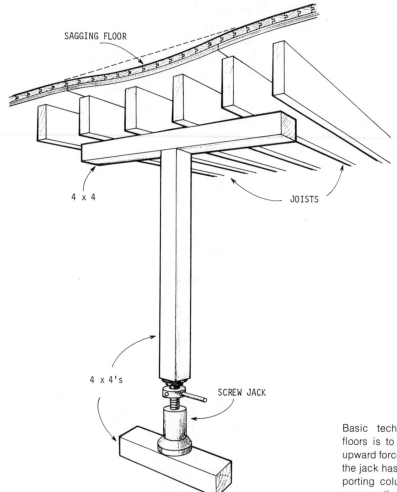

SAGGING FLOOR

4 x 4

JOISTS

4 x 4's

SCREW JACK

Basic technique for fixing sagging floors is to use a screw jack to exert upward force under several joists. When the jack has done its work, force a supporting column in place. Then merely unscrew the jack.

device is a pair of heavy pipes, one of which telescopes inside the other. It can be adjusted to the proper column height, then converted into a jack with an insert at the top with threads and provision for a twisting rod.

When you use a house jack, you need a length of 6x6 to reach from the top of the jack to the floor above, plus a piece of 6x6 long enough to reach across as many joists

as contribute to the sag. If the hoist is minor, you can use a length of 4x4 or two or three planks in a sandwich instead of the 6x6. Also, if the base below the jack is not solid, you need a short piece of timber to act as a pad so the jack won't sink.

When the jacking unit is in place, raise the sag gently. Watch the movement of structural members, noting where the raising is causing movement. By careful obser-

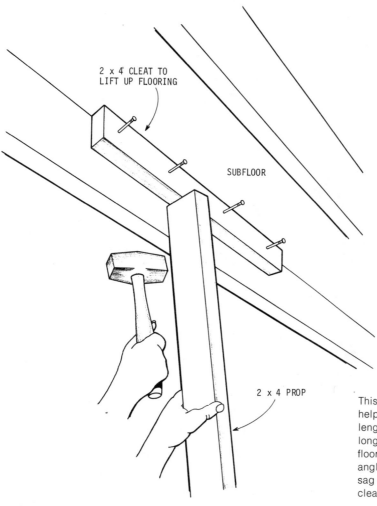

2 x 4 CLEAT TO
LIFT UP FLOORING

SUBFLOOR

2 x 4 PROP

This method raises slight sags and helps with squeaks. Cut a cleat to length. Cut a 2x4 prop 2 or 3 inches longer than the distance from the floor to the cleat. Set the prop at an angle and hammer it over until the sag is corrected. Then just spike the cleat in place.

vation, you can determine which reinforcing and bracing techniques will handle the problem best.

When the jack has forced the floor back to the proper level, spike pieces of plank the width of the joists to the existing joists. These pieces should be long enough to extend at least 3 feet on both sides of the sagging area.

Another method of floor leveling that may be useful involves these steps:

1. Set up the jack so that it rises under the subfloor, between the joists. Put a "cushion" of ¾-inch plywood or equivalent about a foot square on the jack.

2. Raise the sag of the floor, applying pressure gently.

3. When the sag has been pushed out, slip "shims" of wood on top of the joists, in the space between them and the subfloor.

4. Release the jack and let the floor settle back on the shims.

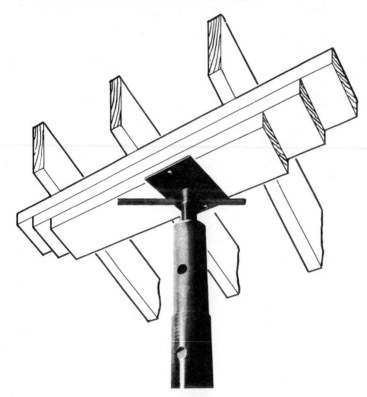

Top of a TelePost is shown here, with its jack and plate under a cushion composed of several lengths of 2x6.

Repeat this several times in the area, if necessary, to remove the sag entirely.

Handling ceiling-floor sags. When a floor that is also a ceiling sags you must decide how much of a blemish it is in your home. Live with it, if you can. If not, fix it.

Remove the ceiling material and use the jacking techniques covered above, reinforcing the joists as required. Use a 4x4 or 6x6 across the joists of the floor you are jacking from, to distribute the weight.

An alternative is to remove the flooring and subflooring from the floor above, in the area of the sag. Cut straight and true 2x4s long enough to span the area. Spike these 2x4s to the existing joists, so that they represent the new bearing surface for the flooring, true and level. Replace the flooring.

HOW STAIRS ARE BUILT AND MAINTAINED

The stairways in your home must be considered part of the overall floor system. In most cases, stairs are the product of specialty woodworking shops. They are prebuilt to meet the specifications of the house in which they are to be installed. Joinery is precise. The selection of materials is meticulous. They are built to last. But, like floors, they develop squeaks. The treads often wear because of the concentration of traffic.

Often stairs may be assembled and installed without glue, since the careful cabinetwork at the stairworks makes interfitting joints strong enough to last without adhesives. Therefore, introducing glue to joints that squeak or wear loose is often a quick and easy remedy for stair problems. This would include all joints between treads and risers, and between stair components and moldings, or cleats running parallel to riser and treads. Glue might help between the tread-riser units and the stringers, but there is a chance that differences in cross-grain expansion and contraction would destroy the effectiveness of the glue.

Despite the greater woodworking strength of rabbeted stair construction, there is a somewhat greater probability of squeaks, because more surfaces meet. On the other hand, virtually the only likelihood of squeaking in stairs with butt construction is where the tread fastens to the bottom of the riser.

Details for eliminating squeaks in both types of construction are given in the accompanying drawings. It is interesting and important to note that reducing the noise adds to the strength of both types of steps.

If the procedures fail, the noise may be caused by friction between treads and the stringer. You can fasten cove or quarter-round moldings to both elements, if you can get at them from below. Or, from the top, if this would not ruin the appearance of the stairs. However, a squirt of oil or dry lubricant may be an adequate answer.

Replacing a tread. When household traffic or physical damage makes it necessary to replace a stair tread, the job is difficult unless you can get at the back of the stairs. If the stair is "sealed" your first decision must be whether it is worth the work to remove the plaster or gypsum board or other material that seals the back of the stairs. If (or when) the stair is open in back, these are the basic steps:

1. Remove moldings, coves, and cleats that will come loose. They'll go back—so try not to damage them.

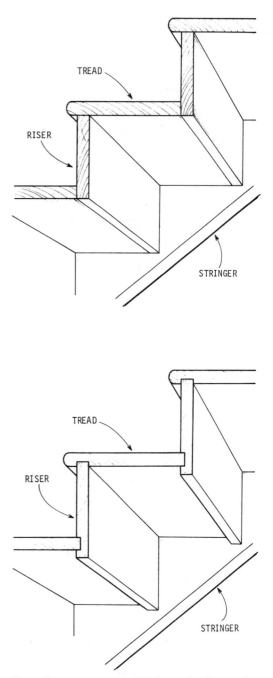

Two most common forms of stair construction are the butt (top) and the rabbet (below). The rabbeted form is stronger, more expensive. Utility steps are often built with 2x8 stringers and threads, with no risers.

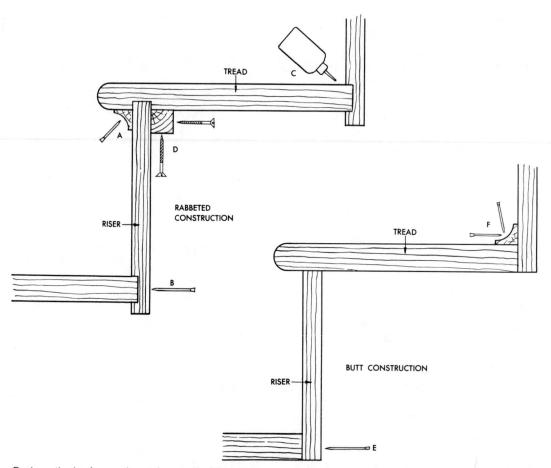

Basic methods of correcting stair squeaks. (A) Nails through cove and top of riser into tread. (B) Nails through bottom of riser into back edge of tread. (C) Oil or a dry lubricant in any of the joints. (D) Cleat nailed or screwed to both tread and riser, underneath. (E) Nail through tread into riser, angling nails for maximum holding power. (F) With brads and glue, fasten a molding into the corner of tread and riser.

2. Saw the worn tread in half in the middle. Be careful not to damage either riser.

3. Lift out the two halves of the tread. In butt construction, this will require pulling them off whatever fasteners come through the stringers into the tread ends. In rabbeted construction, it will involve some fasteners, plus removal of the ends and back of the tread from the grooves into which they fit.

4. Cut a piece of stair tread (lumberyards sell tread that matches most existing stairs) very carefully to whichever of these lengths the situation calls for:

Exactly the distance between risers in butt construction.

Exactly the distance between risers *plus the depth of the rabbet* in one stringer.

Installing the new tread requires some improvisation, determined by the type of construction and the way the stairway is built into the rest of the house.

The butt-construction tread must be fitted between the stringers in the position of the old tread. Before you put it in place, however, screw two sturdy cleats to the stringers, one on each side, precisely at the level of the bottom of the original tread. Insert the tread. If the outside of either or both stringers is exposed, run screws through it into the ends of the tread. If you can get at the underside of the stairs, run screws up through the cleats to hold the tread in place. If you cannot get at the underside, drive screws through the tread into the cleats. Sink all screws and fill the holes with wood plastic or with cross-grain plugs cut out of matching wood with a plug-cutter.

Installing a new tread in rabbeted construction involves a few different steps. To begin with, the tread may have a groove near the front edge which fits over the riser below. The lumberyard tread you buy may not have this groove. If you have the equipment, cut it yourself, using the old tread as a pattern. Or take the old tread and the new to a cabinet shop and have the groove cut. (The original stairworks may be nearby — an excellent source of replacement treads.)

To put the tread in place, insert it in one of the rabbets in the stringer, *the full depth*. It will now fit down between the stringers at the other end, but will not extend into the rabbet. Slowly slide it into that rabbet, until it rests half-depth into each rabbet. Fasten it there, supported on each end. If it is possible, as above, put cleats under the ends.

Replace all the moldings, coves, etc., that you removed originally, using glue wherever possible.

The new tread is now ready for sanding and finishing to match the existing stairway.

14

Flooring Materials

Since the floor of a room is one of its largest areas — and by far the most abused — a great deal of care must be given to the selection of the material that covers it. Not only does a floor play a great part in the appearance of the room, but at the same time it must stand up under heavy traffic. The flooring industry provides us with a selection so wide that meeting the endurance requirements can be based almost entirely on appearance, since some of the most delicate-looking patterns may also be among the longest wearing.

WOOD FLOORING

When man started putting up houses with floors off the ground, wood took over from the stone materials that had, until then, been laid directly on the earth — and that are today making a comeback.

The most common form of flooring is called "strip." It comes in random lengths about 2 inches wide. Although the floor it makes is interesting to look at, whether it is oak or maple, the floor is most often considered functional. In rooms where decoration is important, the flooring may end up under rugs, or even under wall-to-wall carpeting.

There are variations of wooden "boards" for floors, in widths up to 5 or 6 inches, that take greater advantage of the natural beauty of wood. Such boards are tongue-and-groove, like strip flooring. They are usually selected for grain pattern. Some mills turn them out prefinished. Often they are decorated with simulated plugged screw holes, to increase the visual interest. Prefinishing is common.

For porches, you can buy flooring milled from fir, about 3½ inches wide, tongue-and-groove on the edges. The material is also used for utility flooring. At the mill, it may be turned out with the flat of the grain at the surface, or it may be turned out edge-grain. The latter is by far superior from every standpoint.

Some of the rarer woods, including walnut and varieties of exotic tropical hardwoods, are also available in flooring form, usually prefinished.

Although the standard thickness for

Many flooring outlets today have specially planned color coordinating centers which help you determine which flooring material goes best with your furniture, walls, draperies. Many flooring customers bring samples of their existing colors to these centers, to make perfect selections.

wooden flooring is nominal inch (usually close to $^{25}/_{32}$), most of the materials are now available in thinner strips, intended for reflooring work in the main, usually fastened down with adhesives, usually prefinished.

If you happen to live in a place of the "old New England farmhouse" variety, you may want to think of flooring that is actually tongue-and-groove subflooring. It is a fitting choice — rustic and unadorned, with knots and irregular grain. Stained, then finished with a penetrating floor finish, it starts with an old look and grows older with every footstep.

Flooring squares. Wooden flooring in the form of tiles (usually in the neighborhood of

12x12 inches) has become popular both because of its interesting look and the ease with which it is installed. The squares are usually tongue-and-groove, although there are plain-edged versions.

The woods available range from strips of oak to plywoods with facings of the most exotic of cabinet woods. Most of them are prefinished; once the floor is down, it is ready to be lived on.

Installing the squares is simple. They go down with adhesives, which makes them a popular do-it-yourself floor renewal product.

Still another form of tilelike wood flooring is made from manmade materials such as chipboard or hardboard. Rather than

159

Block flooring is often laid in a manner to produce an accented checkerboard effect, as shown in this sample from Bruce. Blocks or squares may be solid wood strips, held together with splines, or there may be plywood with the select wood on the surface.

Exotic woods such as this teak from Wood-Mosaic appear frequently as squares, since small pieces of wood can be used attractively and economically.

square, these floorings come in nail-down strips or units that measure 2x4 feet, often with grooves to look like boards or squares. On the floor, these materials can be stained, painted, or varnished — or simply waxed. (One producer is Forrest Industries, Dillard, Oregon.)

When you shop for wood flooring, you'll find that the typical lumberyard may carry very little in stock, but will be able to show you samples, then order your needs. If you are interested in some of the less common types of flooring or species of wood, it may be best to visit an outlet specializing in flooring. Also, some of the contemporary

paneling centers handle material for floors, or have in their files the catalogues of mills specializing in flooring.

An important consideration when you think about wood flooring is the finish. If a wood floor is finished with a material that coats the surface only, the appearance is no more durable than the finish itself. On the other hand, there are penetrating wood finishes for floors that sink into the wood, transforming a measurable depth of the surface into finish. The wood must wear away to the depth of such finishes before the bare wood begins to show. And this could mean practically forever, except in places where there is much traffic — and especially where the traffic turns a corner.

Sheet materials for floors are made today in perfect duplication of other materials that might be hopelessly costly in their true form. An example is this intricate wood parquet flooring pattern from Armstrong.

SHEETS AND FLOOR TILES

It all began, a few generations ago, as "linoleum." Today, thanks to chemistry, sheet flooring comes in everything-proof materials that look like anything from maple to marble, from teak to tile. Such companies as Armstrong, Congoleum, GAF, and others offer ranges in materials and patterns and colors that give you a choice of thousands of different floors. You make your selection mainly on the basis of color and decorative acceptability; the product's serviceability can be assumed.

Meanwhile, linoleum is still with us, but vast improvements have overtaken the rather dull and prosaic plains and patterns of years ago. The major advantage of linoleum is cost; it is cheaper than most contemporary sheet materials. But it wears well, is easy to install, and can be used anywhere except on floors that are on grade or below grade. Which leads us to the first question you ask yourself when you consider a flooring material: Where is the floor it goes on *located?*

Cushioned vinyl flooring gives you softness and quietness under foot, along with a water-and-wear resistance that makes brick tile pattern such as this Kentile version excellent for kitchen-dining areas, where floors must be both tough and attractive.

If the floor is on grade or below grade, you should restrict your thinking to vinyl sheet or tile, or asphalt tile. Some manufacturers, however, put out other materials — even foam-backed — with a special coating that resists the moisture and alkaline effects that are always present to a degree in concrete that is in contact with the ground.

There is, in addition, a sheet-form flooring material intended for use outdoors, over smooth-troweled concrete.

Inside the house, anything goes on suspended floors — that is, floors that have rooms or basement or properly ventilated crawl space beneath them. The selection, functionally, must be based on the area where the flooring is to be used.

Kitchens, baths, laundries, call for vinyl — preferably in sheets rather than tiles, to cut down on the chance that water might seep through the joints between tiles and eventually rot away the underfloor. With some materials (Armstrong's cushioned Vinyl Corlon is an example) the seams can be made completely waterproof. If you pick one of several floorings that come as wide as 12 feet, no seams may be needed.

When heavy traffic suggests the possibil-

The look of small chips ground and polished smooth (once a common commercial floor surface) appears on this vinyl sheet from GAF. An advantage of such patterns is their ability to make a little dirt inconspicuous, until you get time to clean the floor.

You can spruce up any room in a few hours with floor tiles that press in place, such as these from Armstrong. The design extends from wall to wall — just like more expensive sheet vinyl.

ity of excessive wear, flooring experts recommend one of the heavier gauge materials, intended for tougher duty — perhaps even commercial. They also point out that you should avoid surface-only printed designs for traffic areas. The "inlaid" materials, with a pattern that goes clear through to the back, do not show wear until the material is actually worn out.

However, modern sheet-form materials are in themselves so resistant to wear that appearance and ease of upkeep are the only considerations. And upkeep is less of a problem than most homeowners believe; most of them do heavy cleaning with scrubbing techniques when soft-mop wipe-up would be perfectly adequate. (When you decide on a flooring, ask the dealer for the manufacturer's recommendations for upkeep — usually in leaflet form.)

Another factor may be the degree of noise or comfort under foot. When these qualities are a consideration, do not pass up the materials backed with foam; they are quiet and soft to walk on. Some cushioned sheet materials will lie flat with no adhesive or other fastening. An example is Congoleum CushionFlor.

GENUINE TILE FLOORS

In many ways, genuine ceramic or other mineral-source tiles are the most durable of anything you can put on a floor. That is why they have long been used on bathroom floors and in entryways.

Tiles are produced in a variety of interfitting shapes, in a wide range of sizes, a multitude of colors. Some wall tiles are rugged enough for use on floors, making a perfect match between walls and floors in baths.

There are, also, tiles in perfect imitation of bricks—some of them, in fact, baked in the same way as bricks, but only a half-inch or so thick, so they can be handled easily and are light enough for floors. Other materials, such as slate, are also sliced thin and cut into tile sizes. Just about every natural material is also available in excellent tile-made reproductions.

One of the most popular tiles for bathroom floors is called "quarry" tile, not because it comes from a quarry, but because the individual tiles are tiny (1x1 inch or so) squares. These tiles are not clay with ceramic baked on them. Instead, they are solid, baked clear through, of a single homogeneous ceramic material.

Genuine floor tiles are not difficult to handle, going down quickly and smoothly with an adhesive. Many of them are "unitized" with a backing that may also provide the grout. All of them are accompanied by

Lay soft-surface flooring on the bathroom floor, for the best in comfort and simple upkeep. Sears stores are one source of the material.

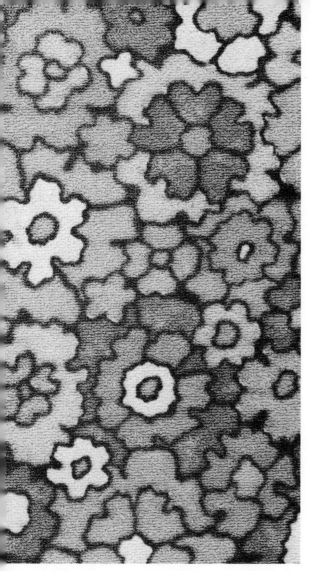

Extra wear and ease of cleaning are features of colorful, interesting printed carpeting, such as the Adventure series from Armstrong.

various special shapes for baseboard coves, inside and outside corners, and other problem areas.

SOFT-SURFACE FLOORS

Soft-surface floors are no longer thought of as interior decorating items handled only by furniture and specialty shops. Scores of patterns and textures are now available in carpet "squares" that the homeowner can put down even more easily than hard-surface tiles.

Some of them are intended for indoor or outdoor use. Some are so water-tolerant and cleanable that they earn recommendations for bathrooms. Anywhere in the house (or terrace), maintenance is easy, since the delicate nature of regular carpeting is gone.

The soft-surface field includes mainly pile-form or loop-form carpetlike material that is not woven, as carpets are. Instead, the pile or loops are embedded in a flexible, tough backing material. Either in tile form or in wide rolls, these flooring materials go down with adhesives.

While some of the patterns follow the general mood of carpeting, there are now soft-surface materials that are given far more intricate and exotic coloration, by means of printing after the "weaving" is finished.

15

Resilient Flooring: Sheet or Tile

Sheet-form flooring materials were once quite difficult for the average handyman to handle. They were stiff—hard to cut, hard to fit, and hard to make lie flat. New materials have changed all that, and today's flooring outlets handle many types that are as easy to put down as tile.

On the other hand, peel-off adhesive backing and other adhesives have made resilient tile so easy to handle that a new floor is less than a weekend job.

The first consideration in working with sheet or tile is the condition of the subfloor.

THE PURPOSE OF UNDERLAYMENT

Although some of the softer and more flexible resilient floorings will "follow" slight irregularities in the floor surface without rupturing, the lack of smoothness may be unsightly. For that reason, underlayment is standard in any tile or sheet job except over surfaces which are smooth and plane. It is usually not needed when you put resilient flooring over a previously tile- or sheet-covered floor, unless the old floor is coming loose. And, it may not be needed over new construction if the subfloor was carefully handled with the flooring in mind. Over almost any old wooden floor, underlayment is essential, as it is over typical subflooring.

Its purpose is to "bridge" irregularities and cracks in the original flooring or subflooring, providing an entirely smooth base for the new floor. When underlayment is done properly, the resulting floor is almost perfectly plane and smooth.

Materials. Underlayment can be hardboard, particleboard, or plywood. The plywood and hardboard are most often used in the $1/4$-inch thickness. With particleboard, you can use thicknesses up to $3/4$ inch, if the condition of the floor calls for extra rigidity that would bridge greater irregularities.

To insure against nail "popping," be sure to use ringed or cement-coated nails. The length should be about $1\frac{1}{4}$ inches for the $1/4$-inch material. If you use heavier particleboard, pick nails that will go through the board and well through the subfloor about

166

In some instances, a subfloor that is not specifically intended for resilient flooring can be brought into shape with special fillers. Use the filler in knotholes, along cracks, and in other areas not smooth enough for flooring.

3/4 inch. In all cases, the nail heads should be "sinker"—the flat beveled kind that drive smooth and flush with the surface.

When there are fairly deep "dishes" in the subflooring, along with large cracks, it may be advisable to use a filler under the underlayment, to level these areas. (Check with your building supply dealer for the recommended filler; the common kind used on walls will not do the job.) In some kinds of irregularity, it may be necessary to plane off high spots.

Nailing techniques. It is extremely important for underlayment to be fastened down securely. That is the reason for ringed or cement-coated nails; their holding power is great, particularly the ringed version. Spacing is critical, too.

Nails should be spaced every 6 inches in both directions when you work with hard-board. They should never be driven closer than 3/8 inch from the edges of the material. Whenever possible, nails should hit joists, for the greatest firmness and holding power. The same spacing is adequate for plywood.

When thicker particleboard is the underlayment, you can drive nails every 10 inches across the field, every 6 inches along the edges, but never closer than 1/2 inch from the edge.

The actual nailing calls for two precautions. First, do not expect the nail to carry the underlayment into contact with the subfloor. Instead, apply enough downward pressure with the free hand—or by stepping close to the nail—so that the sheet is held down against the subfloor.

Also, drive the nails so that the last blow takes the top of the sinker head exactly flush with the surface. Avoid the "dimpling" that is sometimes desirable when

Special hammer-driven staplers speed the job of putting down underlayment. Rent the gun from your flooring dealer, and buy special staples that spread as they are driven into the subfloor.

you drive nails; the dimple could, over a period of time, become visible as a slight depression in the flooring.

Staples can be used for underlayment, driven with a stapling hammer or gun, but the process does not give the holding power of ringed nails. (Check with your dealer for stapling recommendations for the particular material you use; he will probably be able to rent you a stapling gun.)

Special sealers. Whenever a floor is over a crawl space that does not, itself, have a vaporproof floor, you should use a layer of moisture-vapor barrier film over the subfloor, before you put down the underlayment. This prevents excessive moisture from causing early damage to the underlayment and possibly to the final flooring.

Arrangement of sheets. The length of the 4x8 sheets should lie across the subfloor if it is plywood. They should lie across the floor joists if the subfloor is in strips. They should lie across existing wooden flooring. These arrangements guarantee the greatest interlock between the underlayment and the subfloor.

Before you start putting the underlayment down, it is necessary to remove the shoe molding—the strip that runs along the bottom of the baseboard. Unless the molding is ruined when you remove it, you can nail it back after the flooring is in place. The thickness of the underlayment plus the flooring will raise it high enough to cover the break in the baseboard finish.

You must always allow about $1/8$ to $1/4$ inch space between the sheets and the walls. Between sheets, across the floor, about $1/16$ inch is recommended—about the thickness of one of your flooring nails. This spacing allows for a certain amount of expansion and contraction of the sheets with changes in temperature and humidity.

Avoid spaces between sheets that form a cross. In other words, if you start one row with a full sheet, start the next row with a half sheet. This puts the lateral joints halfway along the long edges of the sheets.

The above procedures should make it possible to avoid a joint in the underlayment from coinciding exactly with a joint in the subfloor, but if such a coincidence should occur, trim enough off the underlayment sheet to put the joint over a board—not a crack. This may seem like a tedious and pointless effort, but it is insurance against the later development of a crack that would extend through to the top of the flooring.

One more important tip: before you start nailing underlayment to the floor, stand it against the walls of the room with air space

Example of difficult floor layout is shown here. Note how the pattern breaks at the edges, including islands, peninsulas, and other "intrusions" upon the rectangular.

on both surfaces, so that it can adjust to temperatures and humidity. This will prevent undue shrink-and-swell after the material is in place. Whenever possible, avoid putting underlayment down during extremely humid weather, or in conditions that are extremely dry.

New Flooring over old. The ease of application of sheet — and particularly tile — flooring has brought about a great many reflooring jobs that are intended more for modernization than for the replacement of a worn-out area underfoot. In many cases, the old floor is, physically, in good shape. However, if the floor is old, chances are it has been waxed scores of times, and there may be not only a wax build-up, but a wax

penetration. This is most likely with old asbestos or linoleum floors.

When your old floor is in this condition, it is strongly recommended that you use a disc sander to abrade the surface, so that the adhesive you are using has some "tooth" to adhere to. It is necessary to do this sanding only on the areas where adhesion is critical. When using flooring material that is stuck down only around the edges, for example, only the edges of the floor need to be abraded.

Over concrete. A great many resilient floorings can be used over concrete, some of them without special preparation, some with a form of primer to seal out moisture and arrest the chemical action from the concrete. The surface must, of course, be smooth. If the concrete was not troweled smooth, if it has developed roughness since it was laid, or has cracks, filling is essential. A special latex-formula filler does the job. Check with your dealer for the material recommended for the tile or sheet you plan to use.

WORKING WITH FLOORING IN ROLLS

Sheet-form flooring comes in rolls that are 6 feet or 12 feet wide, or 9 in some varieties. This is the key factor in determining your needs. Will the 12-foot width go on the floor without undue waste? Would it be better, because of shape and size, to use 6-foot widths? Might the area accommodate two 9-footers best?

The pattern is a factor too. Is the design such that it should be used either in the whole or perhaps split exactly in half where it hits the wall in exposed situations?

The easiest way to arrive at the answers to these and other questions regarding the amount of flooring to buy is to make a scale drawing of the floor. The drawing doesn't have to be exactly accurate, as long as you mark the precise dimensions on each edge. Make the drawing by letting 1 inch equal 1 foot. Half a foot is 6 inches. A $1/4$ foot is 3 inches. Three-quarters of a foot equals 9 inches. And that is accurate enough for your purposes.

Cut some paper into a strip as many inches wide as the roll of flooring is wide. Lay this strip on your drawn-to-scale floor. Try it several different ways, until you come up with the arrangement that works out best.

Keep one factor in mind: Do not allow a seam to fall in the middle of a heavy traffic area of the floor. It would be better to have two seams, one on each side of this much

traveled space. For that reason, it is always best to work with the widest possible roll that will meet your needs insofar as appearances are concerned. In many cases, the 12-foot roll will make it possible to cover the floor without any seams at all, and that is, of course, highly desirable. Some of the materials flooring dealers handle almost "flow" together at the seams with special adhesives, making the joint quite water-and-wear-proof.

When you have determined your needs via the scale-drawing method or any other system, it is best to buy a strip that is at least two pattern repeats longer than the estimates indicate. This will allow you to make adjustments as required at the ends and at the seams for the best appearance. You may end up with a little scrap that looks like waste. Store it in the attic as insurance against a day when a serious accident may require patching the floor.

Cutting the flooring to fit. Tough as today's sheet-form flooring materials are, they can be cut easily with a pair of heavy shears, or with what is called a linoleum knife. Use shears if there is any shape or curve to the edge you are cutting. Use the knife and a straightedge to make straight cuts. Important: Be sure to hold the knife at exactly 90 degrees to the surface.

To determine the shape and dimensions of the materials — if the floor is irregular, not rectangular — follow these steps:

1. Decide which direction on the floor the flooring should run. This will be affected by the shape, the number of seams, and the way the roll can be used with the least waste.

2. Determine the way the pattern should fall. In some circumstances, a whole or a half pattern may look best at a wall. In others, the appearance at the wall may be

less important than the way the pattern falls around irregularities, such as sinks, hearths, and other divergences.

3. Cut the first strip (if there are more than one) to length.

4. Lay the strip out on some floor area large enough to accommodate it—which may or may not be the floor where it will go.

5. Measure very carefully, mark the cutting lines on the sheet, using a soft pencil. It is a good idea to recheck the dimensions, then recheck the marks on the sheet, to make sure you are not about to cut a piece too small. Keep in mind that most materials require a little space at the walls, which is later covered by the shoe mold.

6. Cut the piece to shape and size, following the lines carefully, using a straightedge if the cut is straight.

Put this piece in exact position on the floor, and use it as the starting line for the next sheet, if there are more than one.

Starting with the edge of the first piece as a base, measure, mark, and cut the next piece, using the same techniques as those just outlined for the first strip. Lay this piece in place, butting up against the first one.

At this point, it is a good idea to let the flooring "season" overnight, so that it becomes accustomed to its position and layout. Some of the materials used in flooring have what might be called "plastic memory"—and will return to a former shape and size if they happen to be stretched or otherwise forced out of their natural form.

The foregoing assumes rolls that are actually prepared at the factory with clean-cut edges. In some cases, there may actually be a selvage at the edge which is meant to be cut off when the flooring goes down. If your flooring has this selvage, you must cut it off with extreme care, using a true straightedge; or you can use the overlap method

covered below for a special selvage knife. It also may be that in shipment and handling, factory-cut edges have become damaged, although the plastic-memory factor will often take care of this.

Some flooring—especially the type emulating nonrectangular tiles—comes from the factory with edges that follow the pattern. When working with such rolls, you leave a space between the strips equivalent to the "mortar course" of the tile. Later, this space is filled with special materials by techniques that make it look like the mortar courses over the field of the roll.

Most producers of roll goods suggest that you get a better match at the seams if you switch the succeeding strips end for end. This results in a seam that mates the same edge from the roll, rather than seams composed of opposite sides of the roll. This will not work with all patterns, but provides excellent seam quality when it does work.

If, for any reason, it should become necessary to cut edges that will meet to make a joint, the following technique will give you the best result.

1. Position the pieces so that they overlap where the joint is to be. Make sure that other edges are in the proper location.

2. Using the linoleum knife or a sharp utility knife, cut through both pieces without permitting either of them to move. One way to anchor them is to have a couple of helpers stand on them so they won't skid.

The joining edges, cut simultaneously, will give you a good interfit between the two.

Fastening the floor down. The exact techniques for fastening sheet material to the floor depend on the nature of the sheet. Because of the variety of methods used, it is impossible to state specifics in a book such as this. The pictures shown here are

How to Lay Sheet Vinyl

Vinyl sheet flooring such as Armstrong's Treadway, which comes in rolls 6 or 12 feet wide, is flexible enough so you can lay it out in approximate size over the flooring area to determine positioning.

After the flexible material is roughed into position, you can cut it easily and accurately with a utility knife. The steel carpenter's square shown here holds the flooring flat and gives you a straight edge.

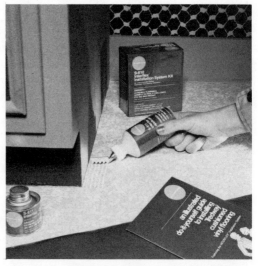

The sheets need to be fastened only at the edges — either with an ordinary staple gun, or with an adhesive. Use the staples wherever there is room, where there will be a shoe mold to cover the staples. Use the adhesive in such places as the toe space around sinks and counters, or where there is no molding. Check your dealer for special adhesive in a self-dispenser.

typical for one of the most common and newest flooring materials, and are intended to illustrate some of the steps in the procedure. The dealer from whom you buy your floor will give you the proper installation instructions, usually provided in leaflet form by the manufacturer. If a roller is part of the process, he can rent you one. If adhesives are involved, be sure they are the kind—even the brand name—recommended by the flooring maker.

One of the most convenient adhesives to use is the double-face tape often used to hold soft-surface carpeting in place. The tape has a "parting medium" on one side. You unroll it, press it in place on the floor, then peel off the parting medium. When the flooring comes down into contact with the tape, it sticks. Be sure it is properly positioned before you apply any pressure.

If your flooring calls for a mastic that must be spread, it is extremely important to spread it properly. In some cases, there may be nothing more than a smear 6 inches or so wide along the edges. With other floorings, the spread may cover over the entire field. When this is the case, the spreader recommended will be notched with a sawtooth edge. The width and the depth of these teeth determine the amount of adhesive spread. Be sure that you use the spreader specifications recommended by the flooring manufacturer or the adhesive manufacturer.

Once the flooring is down, you only have to replace the shoe molding. If you can use the old molding, it saves money and shopping time. If you must use new molding, you'll find it a handy and labor-saving trick to paint it with the primer and one topcoat before you nail it in place. Then, after you have sunk and filled the nails, feather a coating of topcoat over the filler. A final overall coat may not be necessary.

When an over-all adhesive is specified, it is most easily spread with a "toothed spreader," in the shape of a smooth trowel, but with notches cut out of two of the four edges. The size of the notches determines the thickness of the adhesive spread.

WORKING WITH FLOOR TILE

Preparation of the floor, including underlayment, is the same for floor tile as it is for sheet-form materials. The techniques of laying the floor differ only in that you are handling small units rather than sheets, and that you figuratively start in the center of the area and worry about the edges last.

By far the most common tile shapes are square, and the most common size is 12-inch. There are, however, tiles that are oblong, brick shaped, and other variations from square. And, the 9-inch-square tile continues in popularity. For that reason, it may be that determination of quantities and layout may cause problems that must be worked out by the individual, to meet unique combinations of tile dimensions and floor shape and area.

Figuring floor requirements. Determining the number of tiles you need for a job involves one or another of several methods of figuring floor area and dividing by tile area. For 12-inch tile, you merely measure the area in feet, multiply length by width, and subtract for projections into the area or other irregularities. For 9-inch tiles, make the measurements in inches, divide the dimensions by 9, then multiply those results together. Other tile shapes and dimensions can be figured by modifications of these methods, a basic technique being to figure the area of the room, then divide it by the area of a tile.

When the area to be floored is irregular, the simplest method of determining needs is to break it down into rectangles, figure the area of each rectangle, then add them together. Alternatively, you can figure the

By doodling with colored pencils on graph paper, you can work out your own pattern for a tiled floor, and at the same time estimate the number of tiles you'll need.

entire area as a rectangle, then subtract the square footage of projections into the room — or add the area of extensions beyond the rectangle.

In any case, it is best to buy extra tiles equivalent to one row in each direction. When the job is over, put any spares away to use for repairs should they become necessary later on.

Planning the tile layout. Only in the rarest of circumstances will a floor turn out to be an exact complement of a row of tiles. Start a run across the floor from one wall, and you'll end up with a fraction of a tile at the other wall. It is not good if that fraction is less than half a tile, from either the functional or the decorative standpoint. Therefore, adopt this technique — the one used for all tile planning.

First, establish the "center" of the room.

The same "dry" layout of tiles is used for diagonal tiling, a popular variation. Figure on half tiles at the edge, cut on the diagonal, with a border composed of tiles laid parallel to the walls.

In a rectangular area, this means the exact center. If the area is irregular, it may mean the visual center — the point in the room where the best appearance is essential. From this point, establish lines to the walls in all directions, making sure that the cross point in the "center" is exactly 90 degrees.

Now place tiles on the floor in a row, butt to butt, from the center point to the wall. At the wall, you will end up with less than a full tile.

If the fraction of tile is more than half a tile, you should start at the center with a *joint* between tiles. If the fraction at the wall is less than half a tile, you should start with a tile centered in the middle of the tile run.

Do this in both directions.

After you have established a line in the center of the floor parallel to one wall, use a square to indicate the position of the crossline. Lay tiles along these lines, to the walls, to check whether you use a tile or a joint in the center (see text).

Laying the tile. Before you start the actual tiling, check the subfloor or underlayment to make sure that it is as smooth as you can make it. Sweep and vacuum it carefully, so that no debris of any kind will end up revealing itself as lumps in the tile.

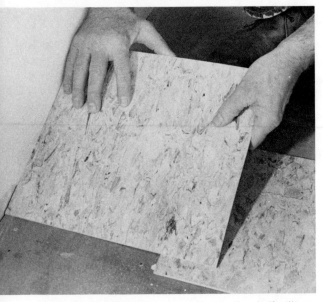

If, at the wall, you end up with more than half a tile, as shown here, cut the tile to fit. If you end up with less than half a tile, switch from a full tile to a joint at the center (see text).

Once you have gone through the dry runs outlined above, you are ready to put tile on the floor. The best way to do this is to lay one strip across the area the long way. Be absolutely sure that this row is straight and true. Use a string drawn tight across the floor to establish the line. Better still, use a chalkline hardware stores sell. Snap the line to give yourself a straight line to work with.

When this first row of tiles is in place, go back to the middle and work in pyramid form. Lay a tile, then two more, one on each side. Put another tile against the first one—then one in each of the resulting corners. Continue in this pyramid manner until the "peak" reaches the wall.

Now work on one side of the pyramid until that side is finished, then move over to the other side. This procedure will make it easier for you to maintain a true interfit of the tiles.

Common practice is to lay the entire floor of complete tiles, then cut the less-than-full tiles for the edges.

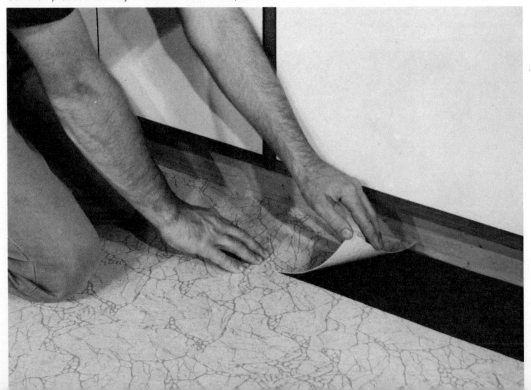

When you lay tiles over spread adhesives, you may find it convenient to stand on the tiles already in position, so that you can place succeeding tiles carefully butted against the previous tiles.

Important: Be sure that every tile butts snugly against its two mating tiles. Since they are produced true and square at the factory, this careful fitting insures a true and square floor.

In the foregoing discussion of putting tile on the floor, no mention was made of adhesives because adhesives and adhesive methods vary greatly. If you are working with peel-and-stick tile, there is no problem. If your adhesive is one that must be spread, follow directions carefully. *Always be sure* not to spread too far ahead of yourself, or the adhesive may start to set before you get to it with tile. Also, if you are interrupted for any reason, use a wide spackle knife to scoop up the adhesive that is not yet covered, so that it won't harden.

All of the foregoing presumes that you are putting down a tile floor in the conventional manner—with rows parallel to the walls and the entire area covered with a single color and pattern. Most of the variations from square and parallel can be effective without being extremely difficult. For example, if you choose to lay a floor of tiles on the diagonal, the only basic difference in procedure is in that line you stretch or snap to establish the first run. Measure across the short wall. Measure the same distance down the long wall. The line between these points will be a true 45-degree diagonal. Other divergences can be figured the same way.

Working a pattern of different colored tiles (or of special strips that work with tiles) involves planning so that you can interrupt laying the tile when you reach the point where other materials come into the picture. In some cases this may be easiest if you start in the center as covered above, but work in all four directions until you come to a change of tile, work out the change on all four sides, then go on with the

Feature strips and other decorative items enable you to design floors to your own taste. This floor is by Azrock, an example of the attractive results strips can produce using relatively plain vinyl asbestos tile.

regular tile. More exotic designs must, of course, depend on your ability to work out laying details.

By far the easiest and most interesting way to work out floor patterns of your own is with graph paper sold at art or stationery stores. Pick the one with ¼-inch squares. Let each square represent a tile. With colored pencils, develop the arrangement or pattern that suits you. Follow the pattern when you lay the tiles. If you are interested in a design that doesn't parallel the walls, cut the graph paper at an angle that matches the pattern and angle you have in mind.

REPAIR AND MAINTENANCE OF RESILIENT FLOORING

It is extremely difficult to repair wear or other physical damage to sheet-form or tile flooring that is very old, perhaps dating back to the days when it was called "hard-surface." The reasons for the difficulty are various. For one thing, there are bound to be color changes, so that even if you use a piece of the original material the patch may be unsightly. In heavy traffic areas, the old stuff may be so badly worn that there would be a notable difference in thickness between it and the new patch. The old flooring may be so brittle and hard that it is difficult or impossible to cut with a clean, smooth edge.

For these reasons, it may be best to consider one of the new materials and a complete reflooring if an aged floor seems to be approaching its tired end.

An alternative, if it would work, would be to remove the worn flooring in a specific shape or area, then replace it with another

178

pattern or color that would go with the overall scheme of things. An example might be a badly worn area in front of the kitchen sink. You might cut out a square "island," oval, or some other design and replace with new flooring.

Resilient flooring of recent manufacture presents fewer problems—including a greater wear resistance to begin with. Physical damage is the most likely cause for repairs. Someone drops a cleaver on the floor or a hot soldering iron. Cut out the damaged area (see below) and replace it with new material, or lift the damaged tile and replace it with a new tile.

Matching pattern in repairs. When you can replace a damaged resilient tile with another, there is no matching problem. With sheet materials, it is different. Here is a relatively simple way to do it:

1. Cut a piece of the same material a little larger than the damaged area.

2. Lay this piece on the floor over the damage and jiggle it around until the pattern at its edges matches up with the pattern of the existing floor.

3. Cut pieces of carpet tape (or other two-faced self-stick tape), raise first one edge, then the others of the patch piece and put the tape beneath it, to keep it in place.

4. Use a linoleum knife or a heavy-duty utility knife to cut through both the patching piece and the floor, just inside the edges of the patching piece. This cut does not have to be straight; in fact, it is sometimes better if it wanders slightly, so as to avoid conspicuous straight lines.

5. Lift the patch and throw away the scrap from around the edge.

6. Dig out the damaged flooring. You may discover that you didn't cut through it entirely in places. If so, carefully follow the cutline with the linoleum knife until the cut is complete. Scrape away any adhesive material that may remain on the subfloor or underlayment.

7. Using the same adhesive methods as were recommended for the flooring originally, fit the patching piece back into the cutout space. Smooth it down. Clean up any adhesive around the edges.

Your patch will barely show.

Maintenance and upkeep. Although resilient flooring once required constant waxing as a means of providing a good-looking—and wear-resistant—surface, many makers of today's flooring insist that the gloss of their vinyl flooring lasts, and doesn't need waxing. Polish, yes—wax, no. Keep it clean, they say, and the shine will continue because the floor doesn't wear dull. Use only a mild detergent.

Actual maintenance, however, varies from product to product, and it is a good idea to follow the manufacturer's recommendations for day-to-day upkeep.

16

Installing Strip and Parquet Floors

The time and labor factors involved in putting down a wood floor range from the slow, tedious matter of laying strip flooring a board at a time to the fairly speedy job of laying wide strip flooring and the even easier job of fitting squares together with an adhesive. Things move along fastest when the flooring is prefinished, yet floor finishing is, in itself, the simplest aspect of the entire job.

SUBFLOOR REQUIREMENTS

If your flooring choice is one of the strip materials, the subfloor requirements are simple. The strips are very strong and will put stability into a floor which may not have had it built in adequately during the basic construction. On the other hand, thin flooring strips, intended for adhesive laying, need careful preparation.

Strip flooring. Put it down over any sound subfloor. If the subfloor is boards, make sure they are nailed securely. If you are putting down a subfloor yourself, follow the flooring industry's recommendations.

Use 1x6 — never any wider — square-edged boards. Leave a ¼-inch space between boards. Nail into every joist with two 10-penny nails. Every end must fall over a joist.

Most important of all, lay the subflooring at a 45-degree angle to the joists. That way, strip flooring can be laid at right angles to the joists without any overlapping of joists between the flooring and the subfloor.

Subflooring of plywood is also recommended, in ½-inch or heavier grades. If you can find it in your area, use plywood subflooring that is tongue-and-groove. Lay the sheets across the joists, with the ends meeting over a joist. Stagger the sheets to

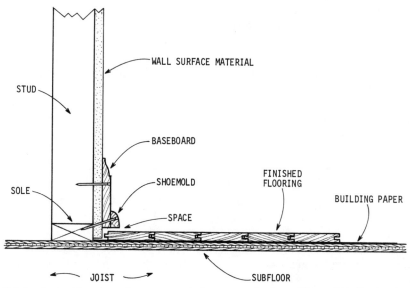

WALL SURFACE MATERIAL

STUD

BASEBOARD

SHOEMOLD

SOLE

SPACE

FINISHED FLOORING

BUILDING PAPER

JOIST

SUBFLOOR

This is a typical floor-to-wall arrangement of components of wood floors. Strip flooring is shown; the same elements are involved when you lay block or parquet. If your choice is thin-strip material, you may need an underlayment of plywood or hardboard to level and smooth the base.

avoid continuing end joints along a joist. Nail every 6 inches into joists, using 8-penny nails, preferably ringed or spiral.

If an existing subflooring happens to be nailed at right angles to the joists, your best bet is to use underlayment, as covered in the preceding chapter. This will bridge any objectionable cracks in or between boards in the subfloor, and eliminate the chance that subfloor joints and flooring joints will coincide, producing a weakness. On the other hand, if the subflooring is of good quality and if it is laid tightly, you may be able to produce a good floor without any underlayment.

When you use the wider strip flooring (3 inches or more in hardwood, and even wider in some primitive or exotic planks), the subfloor is of lesser concern. Since there are fewer cracks between flooring boards, there are fewer chances that cracks

This is what the end of a typical bundle of strip flooring looks like—a bunch of uneven lengths. The purpose of the random lengths is to make it easy for you to avoid side-by-side joints when you lay the floor.

in the flooring and the subflooring will coincide when they are laid in the same direction. In fact, if the subflooring happens to be the same width as the flooring, you can adjust the spacing so that there are no coincident joints whatsoever.

Thin strip flooring. If the flooring you intend to use is the thin strip material, you cannot depend on it to contribute much to the strength of the floor. Consequently, you must use an underlayment, unless the subfloor is quite firm and smooth, and unless you can put down the strips across the subflooring. Even when both these conditions exist, it is safer in the long run to use underlayment as insurance against the possibility of warping or shrink-and-swell of the subfloor boards.

Parquet and block. Think of these wood flooring materials exactly as you would tile.

Block flooring and parquet come in squares, usually with tongue-and-groove edges. Some are full-thickness flooring, some plywood, some thin tile-form. Laying any kind of flooring squares is basically the same as laying tiles, using flooring adhesive.

Although some of them may be plywood units, rugged and stiff in themselves, the frequency of the joints and their alternation in direction means that they will be affected by any contours or flaws in the subfloor. While flexible tiles might "follow" such discrepancies in gentle curves, the stiff block flooring might "rock" over high spots, producing an unsatisfactory underfoot situation.

Therefore, underlayment is almost essential. It is best to use the stiffer, more rigid materials, such as plywood or particle board at least $\frac{1}{2}$ inch thick. Again, the nature of the subfloor is a factor; if it is strong and well done, the underlayment of $\frac{1}{4}$-inch hardboard is probably sufficient.

Cushioning and vaporproof sheets. Both as a means of insuring against squeaky floors and against the effects of moisture-vapor transmission, some under floor situations call for a layer of asphalt-impregnated building paper. The need is determined by three different factors:

● The material.

● The fastening technique. (Nailed-down flooring which doesn't depend on adhesives, for instance, calls for a different vapor barrier from flooring which is not nailed.)

● The kind of space under the floor. (Must you fight the heavy moisture invasion that comes through a crawl-space or an on-grade subfloor? Or, is it in an attic, where there is virtually no hydrostatic pressure to combat?)

Because of the multiplicity of problems in various situations, it is impossible to come up with exact solutions, except through the counsel of a qualified flooring dealer. As you shop for flooring materials, keep the individual problems in mind, ask appropriate questions, and accept the advice of the dealers who stand to gain the most from your overall satisfaction.

HOW TO WORK WITH STRIP FLOORING

The most common types of strip flooring come in bundles, specified as "1-foot," "2-foot," and so on, up to 6 feet or more. This figure designates, more or less, the average length of strips in the bundle. Some of them will be actual length. Others will be shorter.

The area covered by such a bundle is normally *three times the length.* That is, a 6-foot bundle would cover 18 square feet. This figure is only closely approximate, and can be used only as a rough guide to the number of bundles needed to cover a given area.

(The reason for the odd-length packaging is to make it possible for you to lay a floor with no end joints side by side, and to give you short pieces to fill out at the end walls with a minimum of waste. In actual practice, many experienced builders save the short lengths as best they can for use in closets and other small areas.)

Figuring requirements. When you have settled on the specific material you want to put on the floor, check the way it is packaged or bundled to find out how many square feet of finished floor there are to a bundle. It may vary, width by width, type by type. Divide this square footage into the square-foot area of the floor, to arrive at the approximate number of bundles. Note the word *approximate.* The actual requirements will depend on the shape of the area, the way the strips work into the area, the number of runs required, and other factors.

Therefore, you must buy a bundle or two more than your estimates indicate. Dealers ordinarily will not break bundles. Nor will they take back less than full bundles,

should you end up with some strips left over. This is no great problem, however, since you should have a few strips stuck away someplace to be put into service if excessive wear or other damage makes replacement of some strips necessary.

Planning the layout. The first consideration is the direction the strips will lie on the floor. Most often, they will go the long way of the room, since they are best laid across the floor joists, and the joists almost always run across the shorter dimension of the room. You have no problems in the lengthwise direction, since you can cut strips to fill out the run, whatever it may be.

Crosswise planning may be a different situation. Working with narrow strips (2¼-inch or less), most experts recommend starting at one side wall and working across, as covered below. This may result in a relatively narrow strip, ripped to fit, at the other wall, but its narrowness may not be an eyesore in the general pattern all across the floor.

If your flooring choice is one of the wider strips — 3 or 4 or more inches wide — adopt the following procedure:

1. Find the exact center of the room, crosswise.

2. Measure from the center to the adjacent wall — in inches.

3. Divide this figure by the width of the flooring in inches and fractions.

4. If the result is *less* than one-half the width of a strip, you should plan your layout so that there will be a full strip in the center of the room, when the flooring is done. If the result is *more* than one-half the width of a strip, plan to have a joint between strips in the center of the room.

Following these steps will give you the widest possible strip of flooring at the side walls. It must be remembered that all of the foregoing depends on tight application of the strips, along with what must be called normal humidity conditions.

For this reason, it may be just as well to ignore the centering and spacing problems except with quite wide boards. Instead, start at that side wall which will be most exposed to view when the room is finished and furnished. Work across the room. At the other edge, rip a strip to fit, and let it be concealed to whatever extent is possible by furnishings in front of that wall.

When a room is irregular in shape, use the techniques and the considerations covered above, as they apply to edges around the room's irregularities.

One more factor is involved in ideal strip flooring layout. Is the floor exactly rectangular—a true parallelogram? If it is not, the strip at one edge, or at both, will be a long, slim taper. If both edges of the room will be exposed, it is best to establish a line that will divide this wedge in half, making it only half as conspicuous. Do it this way:

1. Find the exact middle of each end wall.

2. Snap a chalkline or draw a string between these points.

3. Lay the first strip exactly parallel to this line. You may start in the center (see below) or you may want to measure accurately toward one wall at both ends of the center line and snap another chalkline near the edge, to work from.

Laying the floor. Assuming that the subfloor is adequate or that underlayment is down, roll out and cement the asphalt-impregnated building paper *across the direction the strips will go.* Lap the paper about 4 inches at the seams. Now follow your choice of two flooring processes:

1. Start at one edge and continue laying across the floor to the other edge.

2. Start in the center and work first to one edge, then to the other.

Either way, you must first remove both the shoe mold and the baseboard all around the room. Do this carefully; you should be able to nail them back after the flooring is down.

If you are working from one edge across the floor, nail the first row of strips about $1/2$ to $3/4$ inch from the wall. You can surface-nail this strip if you keep the nails well toward the back edge, so that the baseboard and shoe mold will cover them when they are replaced.

Two things are important. That first strip must be absolutely straight and true, and parallel to the wall or the line based on the center of the room, as covered above. Be sure of this conformity, because the entire floor is based on that first line. Also, be sure to nail it down with the tongue toward the center of the room, since the tongue always leads when you work with tongue-and-groove materials.

If you are putting down wider material and are basing the arrangement on the center line, you still can start at one edge. However, for that first strip of flooring, you must rip a strip to the proper width to accommodate the width of the room vs. the width of the material.

When the positioning of a joint or the middle of a strip in the center of the room is extremely critical, you can use a special technique involving a "spline." With this system, you start at the center of the room and work both ways.

Nail the first strip in place, either centered on the center line, or with one edge on the center line as the case may be. You can work toward the adjacent wall with standard nailing procedures (see below) on the side of the strip that has the tongue. How about the other edge, the one with the groove?

Cut a spline that is the same thickness as the tongue and twice its width. This fits into the groove of the first strip, and provides a tongue for succeeding strips across the floor. (The spline doesn't have to be a continuous strip; you can rip it from short lengths of flooring if you have them—or from a piece of oak board from the lumberyard—butting the strips end to end as you insert them into the groove of the row of flooring already nailed down.) This provides a tongue over which you can fit the grooves of the first strip in the other direction, and you are again leading with tongued edge.

One precaution is extremely important in wooden flooring; avoid putting it down when it is relatively humid. Never lay flooring in the summer. Do the job after the heating season has started, if you are working in an occupied home.

Buy the flooring material a week or so before you'll need it. Stack it in the room where it will go, and let it adjust to humidity conditions. If you don't, it may shrink after it is laid, leaving you with wide cracks no matter how carefully you work putting it down.

Nailing techniques. Do not attempt to lay hardwood flooring with ordinary nails. Building supply outlets and flooring specialty houses sell special flooring nails. They are harder and slimmer than regular nails. The best kind of flooring nails are either spiral or ringed, for extra holding power.

All these features make flooring nails easier to drive through hardwood without bending, make them less likely to split the flooring, and generally facilitate the nailing techniques flooring calls for.

Except for the first strip and the last—and the last nail at the end of the strip—there is no surface nailing. Instead, the nails go into the V where the tongue meets the edge of the strip.

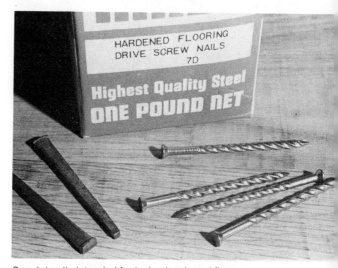

Special nails intended for laying hardwood floors are hardened so they will penetrate the tough wood without bending. They may be the spiral type shown here —or the "cut-nail" variety at the left. Both have relatively small heads so they can be sunk invisibly.

The strips at the wall can be surface-nailed, since the baseboard and show mold will cover it. Note that the tongue edge is exposed—"leading" across the room.

Drive the nails exactly at 45 degrees. Hammer them down until a ¼-inch or so protrudes. Then switch to a nailset.

It is essential, of course, that each row of strips fits tightly against the preceding row. Driving the nail at an angle helps make this a snug fit. However, don't count on the nail to do the whole job. Instead, work out a method of applying your weight to the strip you are nailing, to multiply the friction between it and the subfloor. Use a scrap of flooring as a cushion and hammer the strip up tight, while your weight is still on it. Then drive the nail.

All other strips must be nailed at an angle, into the place where the tongue meets the body of the strip. Use a nail set to take the head flush into the V. Experts often stand on the board being nailed, to hold it as the hammering drives the joint tight.

When strips are bowed, some sort of a lever must be devised to hold them up tight. This technique usually does it—a wrecking bar with the tip against a scrap of flooring (A), pivoting on a fulcrum (B) formed by nailing a scrap of wood to the floor. At the other end of the bar, a nail half-driven into the floor holds the assembly tight while you nail.

Professionals often go a step further. After three or four rows are down, they take a short waste length, lay it over the tongue, then hammer it hard on the edge with a heavy hammer, to drive the strips over tight.

Although it is possible to work across the room two or three strips at a time, staggering the ends, most home handymen find it easiest to work one strip at a time. Work down the row in one direction, cut a piece to fit, then work in the other direction. In some cases, you may cut the pieces from a relatively short length to finish out the strip. In other instances you may find that cutting it from a longer piece will give you a good length for the next end-of-the-row installation.

Important: Be careful not to let end joints in one row fall beside end joints in another row. Experts even work hard to avoid several cross joints close together, even if they do not coincide exactly.

When you reach the side wall, measure carefully, rip the required width, and nail it in place, making sure that the surface nailing will fall beneath the baseboard and shoe mold.

You can, at this point, nail the baseboard and shoe mold back in place, if you are using a prefinished material. If you have been laying flooring that must be finished, wait until you are through with the sanding and finishing before you replace the trim.

FINISHING THE NEW FLOOR

Some unfinished flooring may be smooth enough to suit the style of the room without sanding. In fact, some of the traditional floors such as pine should not be sanded, for a certain irregularity is part of the charm. Some hardwood strip flooring is carefully machined and planed, so that it, too, can go unsanded. For the most part,

however, flooring is not ready for finishing until it has been sanded.

Floor sanding. There is only one acceptable way to sand a floor: rent a professional-size drum sander and buy enough sander sheets to do the job. Use fairly coarse paper for the first run — how coarse depends on how rough the flooring is and how much wood has to be removed to make it fairly smooth. Then switch to medium paper for a second run. End up with fine paper, for ultimate smoothness. Some perfectionists even give the floor a final touch with hand sanding. If you do this, wrap a couple of thicknesses of towel around a brick, and use it as a sanding block.

The biggest problem is the edges. The big drum sander will not hit the last few inches close to the wall. This area must be taken care of with a disk sander. Take the surface down to about level with coarse paper, then switch to medium, then fine to make it smooth. Finish with hand sanding. Work as close to the wall as you can; the trim will cover more than an inch of floor at the edge.

Important. Do not ever run the drum sander across the strips. Sand with the grain only, or you'll never get a smooth floor.

Materials and methods. Floor finishes include oil, shellac, varnish, lacquer, and penetrating sealers. Floors may also be stained, if you're after a dark shade to go with a certain decor.

Oil produces an entirely nonglossy surface, accenting the grain pattern of the wood. It is not a particularly durable finish, since most serious attempts to remove dirt from the floor will also remove oil.

Shellac has the advantage of being fast to use. It dries quickly, and several coats can be applied in a day if the shellac is properly thinned with alcohol. The finish is fairly durable in normal residential use, but may not stand up under severe traffic and cleaning situations. Water resistance is not great.

Varnish has for years been a top favorite for floors, and recent improvements in the resins used make it tougher than ever. You can use a glossy varnish if that's the look you want, or you can use one of the contemporary satiny, low-gloss varnishes. The wearing quality and washability is good, but since the varnish lies on the surface, when it wears through the wood is bare and the contrast with surrounding unworn surfaces is great.

Lacquer was once considered only suitable for professional use. New formulas, slower drying, put it within the capability of the average home handyman. Performance is quite similar to varnish, but drying speed is much greater.

Penetrating sealers are the most desirable of all floor finishes, unless your aim is a high gloss. These materials penetrate into the wood so the finish is not just on the surface. Thus, in order for it to wear off, a layer of the wood must, itself, wear off. This makes the finish the most durable of all. The appearance is very close to natural wood, with virtually no gloss. Waxing is not essential. Cleaning is easy, because of the high water-resistance of the finish.

One last floor-finishing element, once quite popular, not so widely used today, is filler. The open-pore character of oak gives the floor a texture, regardless of the finish used. Many homeowners like the texture because of its natural look, and for that reason, filler is not used with penetrating finishes. If you want a glassy-smooth oak floor, however, you must use a filler. Application is simple. You merely thin the paste filler that paint stores or flooring dealers sell, using paint thinner or turpentine. Brush this creamy mixture on the floor,

working over a relatively small area at a time. When the filler starts to take on a dull look, wipe it off the surface with coarse rags (burlap is ideal). Make all the wiping strokes across the grain. This works the solids of the filler into the pores of the wood. Continue wiping until there are no solids on the surface. Let the filler dry twenty-four hours, then apply the finish. (The natural color of filler is creamy white; if your flooring is dark, you may have to add a little wood stain to the filler to keep it from looking white in the pores.)

Applying the finish. All of the common floor finishes except penetrating sealers are applied in basically the same way. It is a matter of brushing the material on smoothly, in two or more relatively thin coats. Light hand-sanding between coats will improve smoothness and adhesion.

Use a wide brush, but work in narrow strips along the direction the flooring lies so that you can come back and start the next strip before the previous run starts to dry. This prevents an undesirable build-up at the edges. It helps to "feather" the edge of the strip of finish. Varnish, which is relatively slow to dry, can go down in fairly wide runs. Lacquer calls for narrower strips. Shellac dries so quickly that it makes the entire process most difficult.

Penetrating finish is easiest of all to work with. You don't have to brush it out carefully. Just spread it around. Let it penetrate for a while, then wipe the excess off the surface. You can work over fairly large areas, because the material doesn't dry rapidly. After it has been wiped off the surface, it hardens in the wood. You don't have to prestain if you are after a darkened color; the penetrating finish can be tinted, and some outlets carry different colors of penetrating finish, with the stain already there.

It is often a good idea to apply a second coat of penetrating finish the next day, to make sure that the wood has absorbed all it will take. That way, you end up with deep, long-lasting finish that will quite likely never show signs of wear and tear.

HOW TO WORK WITH BLOCK FLOORING

Parquet flooring, plywood blocks, and other square wooden elements are just about as easy to lay as vinyl or other thin tiles. Many of the same techniques are used. Turn to Chapter 15 for information about underlayment, spacing the pattern, removing the trim, etc.

Standard block flooring has two adjacent edges tongued and two adjacent edges grooved. This allows the blocks to be laid with the grain alternating. When you put down the first row of blocks, alternating the grain direction, you get an edge along the row with the tongue and the groove alternating. When you put down the next row, the tongues fit into the grooves—the grooves fit over the tongues, in the reverse alternation.

It is a good idea to experiment with tiles

Parquet flooring squares are composed of regular wood strips fastened into units by means of a spline across the back. This lets you bend-and-break the square into the right size half the time. The squares that hit the wall endwise must be cut with a saw—as must all plywood flooring squares.

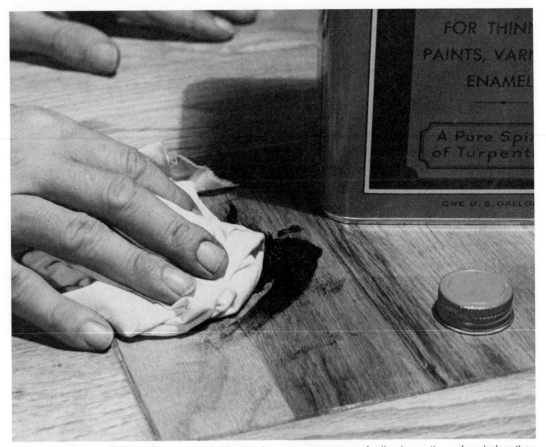

Prefinish on typical flooring squares makes it easy to wipe away any smears of adhesive on the surface before they dry and become a problem.

on the bare floor, until you get used to each tile having an "end" with a groove in it, a "side" with a groove in it, and an end and a side with a tongue.

The blocks can be laid in continuing rows across the room, or in a pyramid pattern. Row after row works best for most homeowners, because they can spread the adhesive all the way across, then go back and lay the blocks.

At the edges of the room, blocks must be cut to fit. Perfect fit is not necessary, since the baseboard and shoe mold will cover a little discrepancy.

LAYING WOOD FLOORS OVER CONCRETE

If your flooring project calls for wood over a concrete slab, the steps recommended by the National Oak Flooring Manufacturers Association will give you excellent results.

First, make sure that there is an adequate moisture-vapor barrier. This can be in the form of a membrane under the slab or floor, if this is new construction. If you are working on an existing slab, the membrane can be asphalt-cemented to smooth, clean-swept concrete. Vinyl film makes a good membrane, or you can use a double-thick layer of asphalt-impregnated building paper, laid in asphalt, with no seams in one layer over those in the other.

Over the floor, lay "screeds" — lengths of 2x4 about 24 inches long. The ends should not butt, but should overlap about 2 inches. Rows should be about 12 inches apart. Mastic or adhesive holds them in place. You'll get the longest life from the floor if the screeds are treated with a wood preservative before they go down.

When the mastic or adhesive has set, nail the flooring to the screeds, following the general procedures covered for strip flooring. It is best to select lengths so that end joints fall over screeds. If you use block flooring, put down a plywood underlayment over the screeds, spread the adhesive, and lay the block flooring as you would over any proper subfloor. However, when the concrete is smooth and level, and when you treat it properly for moisture-vapor resistance, it is possible to lay block flooring without any screeds or underlayment.

REPLACING DAMAGED FLOORING

When excessive wear or physical damage makes it necessary to replace flooring, the job is complicated by the tongue-and-groove character of wood flooring. The easiest way is to use a portable circular saw to cut *across* the strips at both ends of the damaged area. Set the saw to cut as deep as the exact thickness of the flooring. Cut across at least three strips. Then, with a chisel, pry the middle board free. Cut and chisel as needed, to free the rest of the strips that must be removed.

Using new flooring, cut replacements the right length. Nail all of them except the last piece in place, using the standard flooring nailing technique.

The last of the replacement strips calls for this procedure:

Cut the bottom lip off the grooved edge of the strip. This will allow it to drop into place over the tongue of the preceding strip, at the proper level. Since the tongue is no longer available for standard nailing methods, you must surface-nail this last board in place. Sink the nails and fill the hole with wood plastic of the proper color, or standard wood plastic followed by stain.

If only a single strip is damaged, you can replace it if you remove its entire length. Make a saw cut or two down the length of the strip, then use a chisel to pry it loose. To replace it, take two strips whose total length is a little greater than the space to be filled. Remove the bottom lip of one of the pieces and slip it into place, fitting the grooved end over the tongued end of the existing strip. Now cut the other piece to the exact length required, taking the scrap off the tongued end. The grooved end of this piece will fit over the tongue of the first piece, and the square-cut end will fall in place, ready for nailing as covered above.

The foregoing operation can be handled with a single piece of flooring if you can find one long enough, although the two-piece system is generally a little easier.

Replacing damaged parquet calls for the same basic steps as those covered for strip flooring. Saw across the boards in the parquet unit, with the blade set just deep enough to cut through. Be careful not to let the cut extend into adjacent pieces of flooring. Then, chisel out the damaged square.

To put a new square in place, cut the *bottom* element of the groove off, on both grooved edges. The square will then go into position, if you feed the tongues into the grooves of adjacent squares. (The new square will no doubt be a mismatch with others on the floor; for that reason, you may want to stain and finish it to match before you put it in place.)

Part III

CEILINGS

17

Ceilings That Combine Function and Beauty

The ceiling is, in almost every room, one of the two largest areas—equal to the floor. Sometimes, it is even larger than the floor—for instance in rooms where the ceiling is the underside of a pitched roof and in rooms where built-ins occupy portions of floor area.

The ceiling is, moreover, the most difficult area of any room to work on.

For both these reasons ceilings, throughout history, have been the least decorative, least functional areas in the room. It is true that in the days of Grecian architecture, ceilings were edged with coves and moldings and semisculpture. It is also true that in grandmother's day ceilings were carefully decorated with wallpaper, labeled ceiling paper.

Then came an era during which ceilings were painted, in a dual effort to make them inconspicuous and to cut down on tedious

and difficult labor. Buy a gallon or so of "flat ceiling white" and put the ceiling out of mind, if not out of sight.

Today, things are moving backward in ceiling treatment—while at the same time they are moving forward. Although we have not returned to ancient Grecian design, beautiful and not overly complicated cornice treatments are available for ceilings. There is a trend toward wallpaper on ceilings, often designs much more forceful than the quiet papers grandmother selected.

Meanwhile ceilings have accepted such functional assignments as sound control and overall illumination.

HOW CEILINGS ARE BUILT

For the most part, ceilings are not actually *built*. Rather, they are the result of other construction. For example, the living

A ceiling today may combine the installation simplicity of tile with design that complements traditional as well as contemporary decor. The molding that "supports" this ceiling is from Armstrong's modern-traditional line.

room ceiling is really the bottom side of an upstairs bedroom. Or it is the bottom side of a roof.

Most often, the ceiling is applied to the bottom edges of the joists in overhead floors or the rafters in the roof. In many modern homes, however, the joists or rafters may be exposed, with the ceiling material inserted between them. Switch to the most primitive of Early American styling, and you may find fake joists—usually beams—applied over the material that "ceils" the ceiling. (That seeming play upon words really makes use of the origin of the word "ceiling," which dictionaries attribute to the French version of the English "seal.")

The material that forms the ceiling has evolved along with wall surfacing. Origi-

Tile can be functional as well as decorative overhead, as illustrated by these Marlite squares going up over a cracked and damaged old ceiling that would be difficult to repair. Clips nailed through the old ceiling into joists hold the tiles.

Paneled walls and a smooth plaster ceiling go the other way around in this modern interior where the walls are smooth, but the ceiling is covered with redwood V-board.

nally, the area was covered with boards, and today there is a common tongue-and-groove board labeled "ceiling." It's the one that has parallel grooves down the middle, duplicating the double grooving where the boards join. The wooden ceiling is still with us, in contemporary stylings that take advantage of such decorative woods as redwood and cedar and others. Wooden ceilings complement paneling in much modern architecture.

One reason why wooden ceilings re-

Sheet-form materials not only give the appearance of tile, but just as effectively the appearance of wood. The A-frame ceiling is from Masonite; the flat ceiling is from Armstrong.

The suspended ceiling not only provides a smooth look overhead, but can be used to conceal plumbing and other structural features often found in basements and add-on areas.

mained popular for quite a while after lath and plaster became standard wall treatment is that no phase of building is anywhere near as difficult as plastering a ceiling. Yet, almost every home that was built with pride during the early decades of the twentieth century had a plastered ceiling, and more of these ceilings are being modernized today, to cover the inevitable cracking of that old plaster.

The advent of plaster in sheet form changed things. Putting it on a ceiling is almost as easy as putting it on walls. A household handyman can do it himself— although a little help makes things easier (see Chapter 18).

Even easier, however, are the ceiling tiles now available in many different sizes, shapes and patterns. They are light in weight, small enough to handle, and often go up with today's magical instant-stick adhesives. Other tiles are engineered to slip into prefabricated grooves that you nail to

When you want to give the impression of post-and-beam construction, the problem is solved overhead by styrofoam beams with the look of old hewn wood. Such beam imitations are often in channel form, such as this one from Sears, so that electrical wires can be channeled through them.

the ceiling. The result can range from a very simple to highly decorative appearance. Some tiles have a special fire resistance. Some of them, such as the tiles made of Marlite, are completely scrubbable— ideal for the bathroom or kitchen ceiling.

Acoustical treatments. Not only is the ceiling the largest area of a room, but it is also the barest. For that reason it contributes more than any other room area to the bouncing and retention of noises. Every sound that hits a hard ceiling is reflected downward with relatively little diminishing volume. To overcome this, building materials manufacturers have developed ceiling tiles that are specifically engineered to absorb sound, not to reflect it.

In simplest terms, any nonsmooth, nonhard surface refuses to bounce sound. When this principle first came into use, it was for commercial and industrial purposes, and it took the form of square, soft tiles with perforations about an inch apart.

Ceilings designed to control sound reverberations can have an attractive classical look. This Armstrong pattern is typical of a wide range of designs in tile and plank form that go up easily and dampen sound.

Ceilings can be a total source of light, as illustrated by this kitchen-dining area with an overhead framework of light-transmitting Filon plastic.

The sound was absorbed by the tiles and bounced around in the holes. As a result, less was reflected. These tiles were rarely used in residential homes because the pattern is pronounced and not particularly interesting. However, some of the soft decorative tiles now available do their share of sound control and provide interesting ceilings.

(It must be realized that these materials do little or nothing to reduce the *transmission* of sound through the ceiling—either upward or downward. The only answer to sound transmission is *mass*—the actual resistance of the material to vibration caused by sound waves.)

Illuminating ceilings. One of the most satisfying ceiling effects to come along is the illuminated ceiling. It, like acoustical ceilings, began in highly functional units sunk in the ceilings of commercial establishments.

As ceiling lights are now used in residential settings, there is hardly any obtrusion of the light source upon the living environment. The lights are usually sunk in the ceiling, with decorative diffusing elements. Illumination is ideal, yet it seems to come from nowhere, and there are virtually no shadows.

A major advantage of illuminated ceilings is that they can be installed in existing ceilings. The job is simple, using special units that fit between ceiling joists. Even simpler are cove lighting units that you can install at the ceiling along one wall, or along all walls.

How to Put Up a Ceiling

18

When you undertake the job of putting up a ceiling, the first consideration is the ease or difficulty of handling the materials. Gypsum board sheets are the most cumbersome. Ceiling tiles are the easiest to get into place. Boards are easy to put up and may present no finishing problems on the ceiling since they can be prefinished on the floor before they go up.

GYPSUM BOARD CEILING

There are significant differences in the way sheet-form materials are handled on ceilings compared to the techniques you use on walls. On walls, the sheets go on end. The tops and bottoms are covered by moldings, or taped and jointed to the ceiling and covered by molding at the floor. Therefore, there are no end joints on walls.

On ceilings, the sheets go—ideally—across the joists, not parallel to the joists. That way, the ends hit joists. When they are nailed, they present the easiest possible butt joint to hide behind tape and joint compound.

It is essential to stagger these end joints. Do it by starting at one side wall with the first row, and at the other side wall with the second. This, of course, assumes that the ceiling is not exactly 16 feet (or some other 8-foot complement), with a joist conveniently dead centered. If it is, start one row with a full sheet, the second with a half-sheet, and so on, row by row.

The most efficient utilization of gypsum board sheets is based on the arrangement of the joists. In all standard construction, they will be 16 inches apart, on centers. In most standard construction, there will be a joist 8 feet from one wall; in fairly rare situations, the run across the joists may be exactly 16 feet, or two sheet lengths. It may be 12 feet, or a sheet and a half. Probably the most frequent situation, however, will have the "run" across the joists some dimension that doesn't accommodate the standard sheet size so conveniently.

When this is the case, follow these steps:

1. Determine which joist is closest to 8 feet from a wall—*less* than 8 feet.

2. Cut a sheet the proper length so that

one end fits against the wall and the other centers on that joist.

3. Continue across the room, cutting the last sheet to the right length to meet the opposite wall.

This will leave you with a piece of scrap. Is it 16 inches or 32 inches long or longer? Why not start the next row with it? That way you'll achieve the staggered end joints you want, and you'll get maximum coverage from your stockpile of gypsum board. Also, you'll be working more of the time with less-than-full sheets, which are easier to handle.

One situation you may encounter when you start putting up a ceiling is the lack of a nailing place at the walls. If you run into this problem, nail a 1x6 along the wall so you can nail the edge of the sheets up into its bottom edge.

Covering an old ceiling. Gypsum board is frequently used to cover an old and badly cracked plaster ceiling. The only problem is to locate the joists above the old plaster. Since you don't need to maintain the condition of the plaster, you can probe it thoroughly with a spike and hammer, to locate the centers of the joists. Mark them carefully. Snap a line, if they are straight. This will enable you to nail into a firm base at all times.

If you find that the joists above the old ceiling are improperly spaced to accommodate sheet materials, your only answer may be furring strips, 1x2 or wider, nailed on 16-inch centers. Furring strips may also be the answer if your old ceiling is not smooth and level. By inserting shims back of the furring strips as needed, you can level the ceiling.

How to handle heavy sheets. Gypsum board sheets in the standard 4x8 size are pretty heavy and mighty cumbersome to handle overhead. That is why it may be wise to use ³/₈-inch material on ceilings. The thinner sheets weigh less and are easier to work with in every respect.

It is, of course, easiest and best to enlist a helper when the job is a ceiling, but the following tricks make it possible to handle things single-handed. And the tricks work when there is a crew of helpers too.

1. Nail a cleat—a 4-foot length of 1x4—to the wall about ¹/₂-inch below where the sheet will be nailed at that end.

2. Stand the sheet against the wall, and place a stepladder opposite it, about 6 or 7 feet from the wall.

3. Let the sheet tilt forward until the end rests on the stepladder.

4. Get under the sheet and raise it, with the end still resting on the ladder, until you can shove the other end up on top of the cleat, snug against the wall.

5. Position the T (see photos on page 204) under the sheet, out from the wall about two-thirds of the length of the sheet.

6. Start nailing to the joists close to the wall, and when the end is being held up by nails, remove the cleat so that you can nail right at the wall. Keep on nailing progressively toward the end of the sheet being supported by the T. As you near the T, the nailing will hold the sheet up, and you can remove the T.

This same procedure works with the next sheet in the row, the only difference being that you nail the 1x4 cleat so that half of it laps over the end of the preceding sheet. The sheet now going up slides over the cleat in the same manner as it slid over the cleat fastened to the wall.

Nailing and joint treatment for the ceiling are the same as for walls, as explained in Chapter 10.

The problem of holding a sheet of gypsum board up to the ceiling joists is solved with the T and cleat. The cleat, nailed to the wall, holds one end of the sheet. The T, fabricated from 1x2s, holds the rest of the sheet. Below, the T and cleat are used to hold sheets against a slanting ceiling.

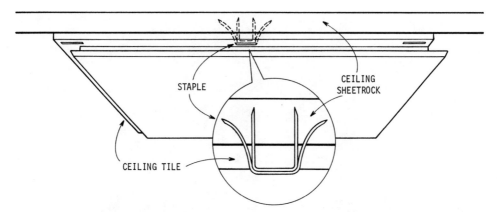

STAPLE

CEILING
SHEETROCK

CEILING TILE

A staple gun can sometimes be used to fasten lightweight tile to a gypsum-board ceiling. Use long staples. Drive one, then without moving the gun, drive another. The second staple will splay, as shown. If your gun won't do the trick, there are special guns for the job.

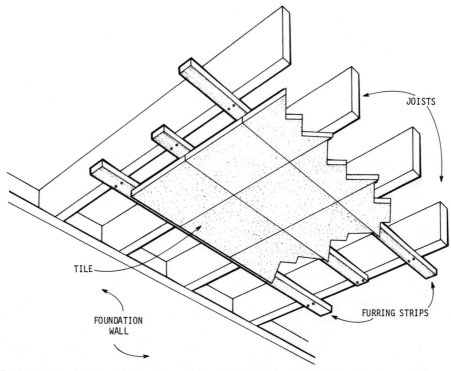

JOISTS

TILE

FURRING STRIPS

FOUNDATION
WALL

Furring strips of 1x2 or 1x3 are the anchors for tile both when joists are not spaced to meet requirements and when an old ceiling is badly deteriorated.

Working with interlocking tiles that go up over joists or furring strips, the fastest and easiest fastening is with a staple gun. Use staples at least twice as long as the flange is thick.

CEILING TILES

Installing ceiling tiles is a far easier job than putting up sheets, for the obvious reason that tiles are lighter, less cumbersome, and require simpler fastening techniques. In addition, there is little or no joint treatment, since tiles tend to accent — or hide — joints in their design. All you need is a suitable ceiling surface to put the tiles on. These are the choices.

Existing ceilings. If an existing ceiling is acceptably smooth and plane, it can usually be used as the base for ceiling tiles. Tiles that go up with an adhesive, however, cannot be expected to stay up if the old ceiling is wallpapered. The paper is sure to come loose. Also, some adhesives (check the labels) may not be recommended over certain kinds of painted surfaces.

Furring strips. When an old ceiling is not an acceptable base for ceiling tiles, and when you are working over ceiling joists that may not coincide in spacing with the size of the tile, the answer is furring strips. Use 1x2 or 1x3 strips, nailed to the joists, spaced center-to-center the size of the tiles.

Grid systems. Leading producers of ceiling tiles base at least part of their line on grid or suspension systems. Although there are differences from manufacturer to manufacturer, the systems involve metal hangers or moldings which you nail or hang up. Then, the ceiling tiles fit into the system without further fastening.

How a Suspended Ceiling Goes Up

1. First step is to nail a support around all four walls of the room at the desired ceiling height.

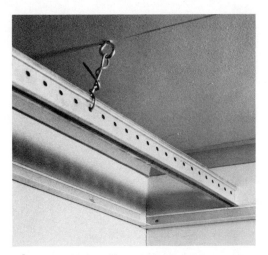

2. Screw-eyes into ceiling joists suspend "runners" at the desired height. Fasten wire to eye first, then insert it through a hole in the runner. With the runner at the right height, bend the wire up and twist it as shown.

3. After all runners are in place, slip the first tile over the molding. Then snap a 4-foot cross-T on the runner and slide it into position to support the tile.

4. Continue across the room with the series of tiles and cross-Ts. At the other wall, cut a tile to fit—and use the cut-off piece to start the next row. (The system illustrated is from Armstrong; you may encounter other systems by the various manufacturers.)

While some suspended ceilings conceal the hanging apparatus completely, others may take advantage of the square-by-square module, using panels that may be 2x4 feet or larger.

Clip systems. One of the simplest and fastest methods of tiling a ceiling is with clips which fit into specially shaped edges of the tiles and fasten to joists or furring strips with a single nail.

Planning ceiling layout. Some ceiling tiles have a design which interjoins visually, tile to tile, so that there is no apparent pattern when the ceiling is up. Others have specific square or rectangular shapes, and the result on the ceiling is definitely a tile pattern. With the former, you simply start in one corner and tile across the area. With the lat-ter, it is necessary to position the overall pattern of the ceiling so that it seems centered on the area. The technique is the same as that for floor tile, as covered in Chapter 15.

In other ceiling designs, there may be a relatively plain or nonpattern tile intended for the edges of the room, while decorative tiles are used across the "field."

When you have decided on the tile you want, you must give consideration to the spacing and arrangement since it influences the positioning of furring strips, grids, suspension systems, etc.

When the grid system goes up without suspension, the runners are nailed to the ceiling. In this case, be sure the nails hit the joists.

The cross-Ts fit over and ride on the channels, as do those used in the suspended system.

The strips or panels covered above can be used in the system, but the runner-and-cross-T system also accepts square tiles of almost any size.

In a modification of the Armstrong cross-T system, when joists are exposed, a clip fastens to the joists that eliminates the need for runners.

Springs hold the suspension grid up against the joists in a system by Conwed. You can remove panels to get at plumbing or wiring above them, merely by pulling down on the springs.

PAINTING A CEILING

Add painting to the list of difficult projects on the ceiling. It is hard to reach. The paint drips and runs down the handle of the brush or roller. But there are tricks that make it easier.

Almost every well-made paint roller has provision in the end of the handle for screwing in a mop handle. This adds enough length to the handle so that you can reach a ceiling with ease. Pick a roller with medium-length pile and you'll get a minimum of drip and splatter.

It is easiest if you put the roller tray on a card table or some other support, so that you can load the roller while you are close to it. Work with relatively small loads to cut down on the mess. Spread a plastic dropcloth under the area you are painting.

Experienced painters start at the edges and paint a strip about 4 inches wide all around the room, using a brush, carefully feathering the edge of the strip. Then, by rolling smoothly and ending with strokes that are almost dry along the overlap at the edges, you end up with a smoother overall job.

What kind of paint? Paint stores carry a special paint for ceilings, usually white or off-white, that is extremely flat. It's purpose is to give the ceiling reflectance but without glare. Wall paint, even when labeled "flat," is not flat enough for ceilings.

A variation—even flatter—is a ceiling paint which contains tiny glass beads. The painted result is a "sand" finish which is particularly well suited to old-style ceilings. Its biggest advantage, however, is an ability to cover and camouflage minor ceiling cracks and blemishes, relieving you of the need for prepaint patching.

19

Beams and Moldings

While your objective may be to make the ceiling inconspicuous, you may decide its large area should deliberately contribute to the design of the room. An increasingly popular method of achieving this is through the use of materials on the ceiling which are commonly thought of as wall materials. More and more ceilings are being papered with bold designs. The kinds of woods produced primarily for paneling (or even for siding) are going up on ceilings. Special moldings and psuedo-beams break the plain monotony of many ceilings, and putting them up is nowhere near as difficult as their important appearance would suggest.

Simplest of all special ceiling treatments must be the use of a shaped molding around the room, a foot or so from the walls. With mitered corners, the molding has the effect of a picture frame. It is most dramatic when there is a chandelier in the center of the ceiling, as is common in dining rooms.

Wooden beams. There are available a variety of nonstructural pseudobeams that have as rugged a look as those used in grandfather's day to actually support the ceiling. Today, the ceiling is supported with standard joist construction, so the beams are purely decorative. However, the look is genuine and the effect is genuinely suited to colonial and some other traditional settings.

You can, in addition, put up nonstructural beams that give the effect of modern post-and-beam construction. Such beams take several forms in today's technology.

Real wood is used to make 4x6-inch timbers in lengths up to 24 feet. They look hewn, but the adze work is done with special grinding equipment at the mill. Cedar is generally the wood used. It can be given a clear finish for a contemporary feeling, or stained gray to look antique. One form of these beams is hollowed out in back, to make installation simple. All you do is spike a 2x4 (the dimension may vary) in place on the ceiling. Then, slip the hollowed-out beam over the 2x4 and drive nails through the sides into the 2x4. The hollow beams are lighter and easier to

Beams of Douglas fir, stained dark, form the support—actual or visual—for this ceiling of western hemlock. Lighting, designed by the architect, illustrates the kind of contemporary design concept now applied to ceilings.

Wood-toned suspended ceiling elements are deliberately displayed, rather than hidden, in this system produced by Armstrong.

The look of hand-hewn wood is illustrated in this beam. The channel shape makes it easy to fasten such beams to a strip nailed to the ceiling.

handle, and the channel offers a route for electrical wiring—and even plumbing in certain situations.

Although 4x6 is the most common size for such beams, they are also available in larger sizes. Also, you can achieve the same effect with 2x6 beams in rooms where the ceiling may be so low that a 4x6 beam might cause headaches.

Beams you make yourself. You can use materials readily available at lumberyards to make beams of your own. A rough-sawn material such as cedar gives a primitive effect. Or, you can use ordinary No. 2 pine, stained or painted to suit your taste. The result will be false beams at the lowest possible cost.

Assembled in channel form, these beams can be put up with a nailing strip. If you use three 1x4's for the beam, lapping the sides over the bottom, you end up with a beam that measures roughly 3½x5. A piece of 1x4 used as a nailing strip is a perfect fit.

Although simple butt joinery gives you these beams with the least work, the result is more convincing if you miter both edges of the bottom piece and the bottom edges of the side pieces. When you decide on this method of assembly, you may find it most efficient to buy the wood in 1x12 dimensions, cutting it to size with bevel rips.

The accompanying photos make the techniques clear. A word of warning, if you use cedar and stain it: the nature of cedar is to absorb liquids, and standard staining methods may give you a darker tone than you want. Experiment on a piece of scrap

cedar to find out how much you should dilute the stain to produce the desired depth of color.

Foam beams. You might be embarrased to know how often you have admired "genuine wooden" beams that are actually foam. The manufacturers use old beams to form molds that accept every character mark of real wood beams. When they fill these molds with styrofoam the plastic picks up every saw mark, every grain texture, every intrinsic characteristic. The technique is used, also, to reproduce the hewn beam effect, and every shape and form of the old adze treatment is reproduced in the foam replica.

Meanwhile, the material weighs next to nothing. You can easily lift 20 or more feet of it into place at the ceiling. A squiggle of adhesive holds it there permanently.

(Shapes and duplications of other materials are also reproduced in styrofoam. Check with your dealer to find out what he can get for you.)

Hardboard beams. Another form of false beams is made of hardboard that is textured to simulate real wood. V-grooves in the back of the hardboard permit it to be folded back, forming a channel with the wood-grain effect on three sides. To put it up, you fasten a nailing strip to the ceiling, fit the three-sided beam over it and nail into the edges. The technique is similar to the channeled beams installation mentioned above.

Ceiling beam arrangement. The most frequent arrangement of beams on a ceiling is in emulation of actual beam construction. They can be spaced evenly across the ceiling from one wall to another. One beam can go across the center with other beams butted into it from either side. This center

Beams you can make yourself, using rough-sawn cedar or redwood, are the least expensive. Nail them together (top) or miter the joints (below). Gentle touch-up with a rasp gives edges natural look.

Among the most real looking of synthetic beams are those made of styrofoam, which make no structural contribution but give a room one of the simplest of all beamed ceilings. This is Lite-Beam, a product of Am-Fin Sauna.

A squiggle of adhesive along both edges of the foam beam will hold them to any ceiling. Clips are also used.

These three photos show how "folded" hardboard beams fasten to cleats on the ceiling and in the corners of the wall and ceiling. Top, a 1x4 cleat goes up, others are already in place at the wall. Center, a folded beam with one side removed forms the bottom and side of the beam in the corner. Bottom, nails through the upper edges of the sides, into the cleats, hold the rest of the beams.

beam may be slightly bigger, to give the impression that it is supporting the ends of the other beams.

This traditional arrangement is particularly convenient when the ceiling is old, rough plaster. The beams seem a logical part of the old ceiling, and as a result you may be spared the tedious job of repairing the overhead area.

Many times the beams go over newly applied gypsum board, and cut down on the need for joint treatment. The preceding chapter stated specifically that the *butted ends* of the 4x8 sheets should be staggered, to avoid a conspicuous run of the butt joints, which are the most difficult to hide with tape and joint compound. If your overhead thinking should include false beams, however, you can make the butted joints up, and put a beam over them. Then, you only have to treat the edges, where standard gypsum board is thinner. One sure work-saver: Paint the ceilings before you put up false beams, and you won't have to bother cutting along the edges when you paint.

Other molding treatments. Moldings of various shapes that are intended for mounting flat on the surface can be used to make ceilings more dramatic. Use them around the circumference of the room, as suggested above. Use them to create a grid. Or use them to cut a ceiling area into quarters or halves.

You can be your own designer. Suppose, for example, that you would like a 4x4 grid of ceiling accent, formed by applying moldings to the ceiling on squares. Suppose that 4-foot squares would be ideal. You now find yourself with no joint problems with gypsum board. Put the sheets, with end joints coinciding. Run molding down the edge joints, and across the end joints, and across the center, using either mitered or coped joints. You end up with a ceiling that has a 4-foot grid, and there are no joint problems. Modify this application to produce any ceiling pattern that suits your needs.

20

Ceilings That Light Up a Room

One of the most modern ideas in ceiling treatment must be considered a direct descendant of one of the most traditional ideas: the skylight. No longer is the skylight a blessing in lighting accompanied by a curse in leaking. Improved construction methods, utilizing improved light-transmission material, make the skylight quite weathertight. Add to that the effect of artificial light planted so subtly and efficiently in ceilings that the lighting is part of the decor, not just part of the illumination.

Lights for ceilings come in many forms. One company — Lightolier — shows twenty-two different variations. Some ceiling fixtures are completely recessed. Some descend an inch or so below the ceiling, enclosed in a bezel or frame. Some might be called modern-day variations on the old chandelier. Some are equipped with swivel features, so that the light can be directed where it is needed — away from where it is not wanted.

INSTALLING RECESSED LIGHTS

Some ceiling lighting fixtures are intended for installation during actual ceiling construction. The frames and housing are made to fit joist spacing. The most common procedure is to fasten the housing in place before the ceiling material goes up. Openings left in the sheets or tiles fit around the housing. Then, the reflectors, sockets, etc., go in, followed by the bezel or frame. That way any roughness in the ceiling opening is covered.

The bezel is usually fastened in place with screws — or with hinges and one screw, to allow for replacement of burned out

Installing a Recessed Light Fixture

1. Fasten the mounting frame between the joists.

2. Install the ceiling panel, with fixture hole cut.

3. Snap the reflector-trim into the socket holder.

4. Insert reflector-trim into the opening and twist.

Photos courtesy of Lightolier

bulbs or tubes. This feature also simplifies painting around the ceiling fixtures, since the bezel can be lowered to eliminate the need for cutting around it.

Since there are many different methods of housing the lights and of mounting the housings, it is impossible to cover them all in this book. The accompanying photographs illustrate the basic simplicity that is common to most systems. Whatever fixture you decide upon will, moveover, be accompanied by detailed instructions provided by the manufacturer.

Important: If you undertake any installation of lighting fixtures on your own, check with local building codes and other regulations. In some communities, do-it-yourself electrical work may be illegal. However, you may be able to take care of the mechanical aspects of installing the fixtures, and then let a licensed electrician hook them up. It may be perfectly acceptable for you to exchange an old lighting fixture in the ceiling for a new one, using the same electrical wiring.

LIGHTS IN EXISTING CEILINGS

You can cut a hole in an existing ceiling and insert a lighting fixture designed specifically for this method of installation. Some designs clamp to the ceiling material. Other, larger units fasten to the joists. The mechanics of putting them in place are easy. The problem begins with the electrical runs. It may be necessary to call in a professional electrician not only for legal reasons (see above) but also because of the difficulty of bringing an electrical run to the place where the fixture is to go.

If you do the job yourself, the easiest way is to "snake" the line between the joists where the fixture will be mounted. Bring the line up the sidewall and into this

Replacing an existing light fixture with one that is recessed is simplest of all. Drop the fixture, disconnect it from the electrical runs, then put the new outfit in place. Be sure the electricity is off.

Recessed lights to match up with ceiling tile produce interesting results with minimum effort. First, the tile-size adaptor plate goes into one of the spaces a tile would normally occupy. Then the reflector and socket fit into the adaptor. The unit is then finished off with a bezel. This one, from Armstrong, is made of wood-grained metal.

interjoist space. Hook-up to the power will depend on the existing wiring—most likely in the basement ceiling beneath the wall. A "switch leg" will be necessary, running to the most convenient place for the lights to be turned on. Alternatively, the switch may be installed in the wall where the line goes up, if this would be workable from a living standpoint as well as a wiring standpoint.

Snaking a line. When you snake a line, you pull it by some means or other through a "tunnel" or channel that is open only at the ends. In some cases, you may be able to shove the line through the channel, if the line is stiff enough. This might be the case with BX or Romex electrical lines in the ceiling situations covered above. However, the only way you can get the line through in many situations is by pulling—i.e., snaking it through.

To do this, you must shove some semi-flexible material through the channel. It may be a relatively stiff extension cord. Or, it may be a special snaking line available commercially, but not universally. In some situations, you may be able to push a thin strip of wood, such as a length of thin quarter-round, through the channel.

Most often the tricks are no more complicated than pushing and twisting and wiggling the snake. Be sure that the leading end doesn't have any points or edges that would catch on the walls of the channel. Be prepared to make two or three or more starts.

Eventually, the end of the snake reaches the end of the channel. When it does, all you have to do is continue the twist-and-turn until the end appears in the opening at the other end. Usually this is easiest if you have a helper do the maneuvering while you keep an eye open for the snake to appear.

When it appears, fasten the electrical cord to the snake and pull it where you need it.

In some cases, you may be able to simplify the entire job of ceiling lights through wiring that plugs into an existing socket near the floor, activated by the same switch that turns the socket on and off.

LIGHTS IN SUSPENDED CEILINGS

When the situation suggests a suspended ceiling, overhead lighting is easy to install. In the first place, you can bring the electrical runs in along the present ceiling. They'll be hidden by the suspended panels or tiles.

More important, you will be able, in most cases, to mount a recessed fixture on the suspended sheet. Or you can simply replace a tile with a light of the proper dimensions.

Lighting outlets handle special units utilizing fluorescent tubes that are engineered specifically for incorporation into suspended ceilings. They are of particular value in areas where a good deal of light is required—for example, in a basement gameroom. Another situation where recessed fluorescent lighting is useful is in a room which may call for relatively dim, conventional lighting most of the time, but where more brightness can be switched when it is needed.

Most suspended ceiling systems, such as this one from Celotex, have translucent panels which maintain the uniform pattern of the ceiling, yet produce excellent overhead lighting. The illumination is especially desirable in kitchens and activity areas.

GET LIGHT AND HEAT FROM SKYLIGHTS

It is normal to think of skylights as difficult overhead projects. How do you keep them from leaking? What do you do about the heat intake when the sun shines through transparent or translucent roofs?

None of these problems present any difficulties if you take advantage of basic construction techniques plus some new ideas in materials.

Study the accompanying drawing and you will see that a skylight can be nothing more than a "pan" with a bottom that transmits light inverted over a hole in the roof. To put one in an existing roof, follow these steps.

1. Cut out the roof around the perimeter

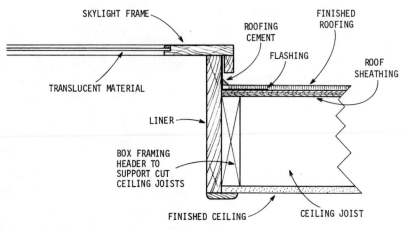

SKYLIGHT FRAME

TRANSLUCENT MATERIAL

LINER

BOX FRAMING
HEADER TO
SUPPORT CUT
CEILING JOISTS

FINISHED CEILING

ROOFING
CEMENT

FLASHING

FINISHED
ROOFING

ROOF
SHEATHING

CEILING JOIST

Schematic drawing of skylight construction that is handyman simple shows: liner around the inside of the cut-out roof; skylight frame that fits like a cap over the liner; flashing and roofing cement that seal the roof around the liner. Be sure to use silicon cement to hold glazing in the frame, for longest life and greatest waterproofing.

of the skylight opening. Follow a rafter on each end (or side) of the opening.

2. Remove the rafters that cross the opening if it is not more than 4 feet wide.

3. Cut a pair of 2-inch planks the width of the rafters the proper length to reach across the opening. Spike through these headers into the ends of the cut-off rafters. If you can get at it, spike through the side into the ends of the two cross rafters. If not, spike cleats to the side rafters and fasten the cross rafters to the cleats (see sketch). Either method will restore the required strength of the roof.

4. If the opening is larger, leave a rafter in the center, or two evenly spaced rafters, as the situation requires.

5. Nail 1x1s all around this opening, flush with the ceiling at the bottom, extending up above the roof at the top. This assumes typical residential construction, with rafters of 2x6s or 2x8s. If the roof is "thicker" than this, cut ¾-inch exterior-

grade plywood in strips wide enough to give you the needed extension above the roof.

6. Using trowel-grade roofing cement, run a fillet all around the joint between the roof and the lining of the opening. This is the key to watertightness, so be sure the cement seals the joint — particularly along the top.

The skylight itself is nothing more than a frame that fits over the opening. Glaze it with glass, with transparent plastic sheet, with corrugated fiberglass — whichever is handiest for you. Or, your choice may be a plastic dome intended specifically for skylights, such as those made by Rohm & Haas. They come with specially designed installation paraphernalia, including gaskets that make things watertight.

What about heat loss and gain? If the skylight is on a southern or western slope of the roof, you'll find that it probably gives you a heat gain, even during winter, on sunshiny days. This is, of course, offset at

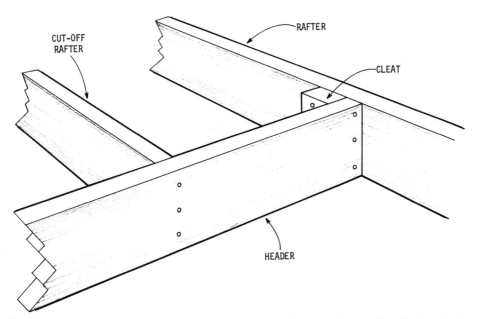

CUT-OFF
RAFTER

RAFTER

CLEAT

HEADER

Drawing shows how headers are spiked to the ends of cut-off rafters. If you can't spike through the side rafters into the ends of the headers, you can spike a 2x4 cleat to the side rafters and then fasten the headers to the cleat.

night and during cold overcast weather. The problem can be licked with the heat traveling in either direction by means of an "overcoat" of 2-inch plastic foam. You'll find that the foam lets a lot of light through — but controls the movement of the heat. To take advantage of the foam insulation on a flat skylight, merely lay strips over the glazing and hold them in place with a grid of 1x2s. The overlay system works only with flat skylights. If you have a dome, you can devise a means of mounting the insulation inside, under the dome, where it can rest on a molding nailed all around the opening.

Index